Radical Feminists

Guides to
Subcultures and
Countercultures

Radical Feminists

A Guide to an American Subculture

Paul D. Buchanan

GREENWOOD

AN IMPRINT OF ABC-CLIO, LLC
Santa Barbara, California • Denver, Colorado • Oxford, England

Library of Congress Cataloging-in-Publication Data

Buchanan, Paul D., 1958–
    Radical feminists : a guide to an American subculture / Paul D. Buchanan.
      p. cm. — (Guides to subcultures and countercultures)
    Includes bibliographical references and index.
    ISBN 978-1-59884-356-9 (hard copy : alk. paper) — ISBN 978-1-59884-357-6 (ebook)
  1. Feminists—United States—History. 2. Feminism—United States—History. 3. Radicals—United States—History. 4. Radicalism—United States—History. I. Title.
HQ1121.B833   2011
305.420973—dc22   2011015401

ISBN: 978-1-59884-356-9
EISBN: 978-1-59884-357-6

15 14 13 12 11   1 2 3 4 5

This book is also available on the World Wide Web as an eBook.
Visit www.abc-clio.com for details.

ABC-CLIO, LLC
130 Cremona Drive, P.O. Box 1911
Santa Barbara, California 93116-1911

This book is printed on acid-free paper ∞

Manufactured in the United States of America

Contents

Series Foreword   *vii*

Introduction   *ix*

Chronology   *xv*

Historical Overview: The Roots of Radical Feminism   *xix*

Chapter One   Publications, Documents, and Manifestoes   1

Chapter Two   Groups, Organizations, and Beliefs   21

Chapter Three   Protests, Demonstrations, and Events   45

Chapter Four   Key Issues of the Movement   65

Chapter Five   Legislation and Legacy   85

Biographical Sketches   *97*

Glossary   *139*

Primary Document Excerpts   *143*

Bibliography   *155*

Index   *163*

Series Foreword

From Beatniks to Flappers, Zoot Suiters to Punks, this series brings to life some of the most compelling countercultures in American history. Designed to offer a quick, in-depth examination and current perspective on each group, the series aims to stimulate the reader's understanding of the richness of the American experience. Each book explores a countercultural group critical to American life and introduces the reader to its historical setting and precedents, the ways in which it was subversive or countercultural, and its significance and legacy in American history. Webster's Ninth New Collegiate Dictionary defines counterculture as "a culture with values and mores that run counter to those of established society." Although some of the groups covered can be described as primarily subcultural, they were targeted for inclusion because they have not existed in a vacuum. They have advocated for rules that methodically opposed mainstream culture, or they have lived by their ideals to the degree that it became impossible not to impact the society around them. They have left their marks, both positive and negative, on the fabric of American culture. Volumes cover such groups as Hippies and Beatniks, who impacted popular culture, literature, and art; the Eco-Socialists and Radical Feminists, who worked toward social and political change; and even groups such as the Ku Klux Klan, who left mostly scars.

A lively alternative to narrow historiography and scholarly monographs, each volume in the Subcultures and Countercultures series can be described as a "library in a book," containing both essays and browsable reference materials, including primary documents, to enhance the research process and bring the content alive in a variety of ways. Written for students and general readers, each volume includes engaging illustrations, a timeline of critical events in the subculture, topical essays that illuminate aspects of the subculture, a glossary of subculture terms and slang, biographical sketches of the key players involved, and primary source excerpts—including speeches, writings, articles, first-person accounts, memoirs, diaries, government reports, and court decisions—that offer contemporary perspectives on each group. In addition, each volume includes an extensive bibliography of current recommended print and nonprint sources appropriate for further research.

Introduction

This book provides two connotations to the term radical feminist. The first emphasizes the feminist arm of the New Left radical movement, including the activities of the civil rights, antiwar, and anticapitalism contingencies. These radical *feminists* were the women of the radical movement, who sought a greater role in these campaigns. These women became tired of their secondary, supportive, submissive roles to the men of organizations such as Student Nonviolent Coordinating Council, Students for a Democratic Society, Mobilization Committee to End the War in Vietnam, The Weathermen, and others. These radical *feminists* quickly realized that their place in the radical left was a reflection of women's place in the larger society. It was a place of limited opportunity, subservient power, and second-thought recognition. The women could no longer wait for the men to lift the oppression that the men themselves perpetuated.

As time went on and the women's liberation movement blossomed in America, the term radical feminist took on a different context. The *radical* feminists became the far left agitating edge of the women's movement. It was the segment of the movement that fought for the recognition of lesbians as a political entity, campaigned for universal abortion rights for all women, and lobbied for equal opportunity supported by government-funded child care. The radical feminists questioned the role of organized religion in the oppression of women, and held up the nuclear family and even the act of sexual intercourse as methods of oppression, and offered celibacy as a viable alternative.

The radical feminists became the envelope pushers of the women's movement. They tested the limits of reform by lobbying for the revolutionary, fundamental restructuring of the patriarchal society, thus motivating the more liberal center of the women's movement to advocate for and accept a wider variety of reforms.

An earlier incarnation of the radical feminists was part of the historic legacy of the Far Left, which dates back to the nineteenth century abolition and suffrage movements, and continued into the twentieth century. Historic figures such as Elizabeth Cady Stanton, Susan B. Anthony, Margaret Sanger, and Emma Goldman predate the radical feminists of the twentieth century as agitators of the patriarchal political and social order. This era is often referred to as First Wave Feminism. It was the period in which women began to define themselves as legal and political entities, out from under the shadow of men. Women sought opportunities in higher education and professional opportunities; legal identity in situations concerning child custody, divorce, and property; and a voice among the electorate.

Many of the radical feminists of the 1960s and 1970s were raised on the writings of Simone de Beauvoir and Betty Friedan. Beauvoir, in *The Second Sex* (1949), brought to light for the first time many of the issues with which radical feminists would grapple two decades later. Meanwhile, in 1963, Betty Friedan legitimately identified the feminist yearnings within the average American housewife.

The radical feminist of the 1960s slowly veered away from the New Left radicals, when the women realized they also were being repressed all over again. Thus began Second Wave Feminism, when women advocated for equal opportunities with men in practice as well as in name. The second wave feminists denounced the oppressive issues—such as limited birth control, media stereotyping, unequal professional opportunity, domestic violence—which limited their full participation in a male-dominated society.

The early years of the radical feminist era saw the emergence of the women's dissatisfaction with the New Left through the release of "Sex and Caste: A Kind of Memo," by Mary King and Casey Hayden in 1965. The founding of National Organization for Women in 1966—which drifted from cutting edge to middle-of-the-road—seemed to energize the radical edge of the feminist movement to create their own collectives. The radical feminists did not comprise a single organized entity, but consisted of numerous women who themselves formed local groups dedicated to the eradication of the patriarchal structure and the liberation of women. The groups employed many of the strategies and techniques learned while participating in the New Left movements for civil rights and against the Vietnam War. The groups included Chicago Women's Liberation Union, Cell 16, New York Radical Women, The Feminists, Gainesville Women's Liberation, New York Radical Feminists, Redstockings, and Seattle Radical Women. Particular efforts such as WITCH and the Women's Liberation Rock Band used the mediums of theater and music to communicate their message. The women began using consciousness-raising techniques, to help the women recognize the oppression in their own lives. Consciousness-raising helped women realize that many of their experiences were commonly shared, making their personal experiences political. However, there remained a continuing struggle between women—known by some as *politicos*—who sought elevated status for women while retaining their allegiance to the New Left movement, and the women committed to creating a separate, autonomous movement exclusively for women.

The nationally turbulent year of 1968 was also the year that women's liberation came to the attention of the nation. The Atlantic City Miss America protest put the women's movement on the map, leading to further events and incidents by which the radical feminists brought their message to the nation. There was The Bridal Fair Protest, in which the radical feminists protested the commercialization of marriage. The David Susskind Show provided for nationally syndicated air time for the radical feminist platform. Valerie Solanas' shooting of Andy Warhol personified much of the rage seething in the hearts of women. The outing of Kate Millett and the Lavender Menace protest forced the recognition of lesbianism by the women's movement. The Speak Out on Abortion event allowed women to talk openly about the previous unmentionable subject. The arrest of Jane Alpert highlighted one woman's conversion from radical to feminist, while the *Ladies' Home Journal* sit-in brought glaring attention to the media's treatment of women.

Many of these radical feminists were talented writers and dedicated researchers and educators, whose findings and theories would inspire generations of women to come. Meanwhile, between 1968 and 1975, the radical feminists produced an astounding collection of feminist literature, which continues to enthrall and influence readers to this day: *Toward a Female Liberation Movement* documented feminists' exodus from the New Left. *The SCUM Manifesto* vividly expressed the rage of Valerie Solanas, and women everywhere. *Notes from the First,* (Second, and Third) *Year* and *No More Fun and Games* became literary journals of the radical feminist movement. *Sexual Politics* and *The Dialectic of Sex* challenged accepted myths of sex and gender, and "Kinder, Kuche, Kirche as Scientific Law: Psychology Constructs the Female" characterized the male-dominated field of psychology as completely inadequate to serve women. "The BITCH Manifesto" turned criticism into crescendo; *The Myth of Vaginal Orgasm* challenged the most basic act of sexual intercourse, while *Against Our Will* addressed the topic of rape as no book had previously done.

With the passage of the Equal Rights Amendment in 1972, and the Supreme Court decision in *Roe v. Wade*, it appeared that the efforts of the radical feminists were beginning to make significant inroads. But these decisions, which in some ways extended the rights of women, may also have taken the wind out of the radical feminist sails. As rights and opportunities for women increased, the need for the radical feminist approach waned. Radical feminism gave way to the middle-of-the-road liberal feminism—which sought to develop empowering reforms within the existing societal structure—and cultural feminism, which created parallel cultures for women that isolated them and insulated them from the oppressive patriarchal society.

Many radical feminists enjoyed successful careers in higher education and the media. Thus, many ideas developed in the era filtered down into the succeeding generation, who would in turn experience as realities many of the rights and opportunities for which the radical feminists had so fervently fought. Some fear that some of these rights—such as the landmark decision in *Roe v. Wade*—may be overturned. Although the revolution that many radical feminists sought fell short of the fruition envisioned, many of the liberties now routinely enjoyed by women of the new millennium can be traced to the protests and struggles fought on the radical edge of the women's movement.

The radical feminist era led to the Third Wave of Feminism—often thought of as beginning after the conservative wave of the Reagan Era of the 1980s. With the Third Wave, the lessons of the 60s and 70s called for a more diverse, and more inclusive, approach. Feminism sought to envelope those from the left and the right of the political spectrum. As the opportunities the first two waves sought finally began to materialize for women, a less combative approach became popular. The Third-Wave also asserted that while progress had been made for women, the war for true equality was far from being won.

Chronology

1839   Margaret Fuller hosts her first *Conversation*.

1848   Seneca Falls hosts the National Woman's Rights Convention.

1849   Elizabeth Blackwell becomes a doctor.

1869   Wyoming grants suffrage.

1872   Susan B. Anthony is arrested for voting in Rochester.

1874   Supreme Court avoids suffrage in *Happersett v. Minor*.

1875   The "Molly Maguires" are formed in Pennsylvania.

1895   *The Women's Bible* is published.

1898   Charlotte Perkins Gilman releases *Women and Economics*.

1901   Emma Goldman is arrested in Chicago.

1913   500,000 watch the Women's Suffrage Procession and Pageant in Washington, DC.

1916   The National Women's Party is created.

1916   Margaret Sanger opens a birth control clinic in New York.

1917   Jeanette Rankin is elected to Congress.

1917   Alice Paul is arrested.

1917   Thirty-three suffragists face the "Night of Terror."

1919   The League of Women Voters is formed.

1919   The Susan B. Anthony amendment is passed.

1920   The American Civil Liberties Union is founded.

1923   The Equal Rights Amendment is launched.

1925   Nellie Taylor Ross becomes governor of Wyoming.

1950   Althea Gibson competes in the U.S. Open.

1956   C. Wright Mills publishes *The Power Elite.*

1956   Autherine Juanita Lucy enrolls at the University of Alabama.

1960   The SNCC is formed.

1962   SDS publishes "Port Harbor Statement."

1963   Betty Friedan publishes *The Feminine Mystique.*

1964   Congress passes the Civil Rights Act.

1973   Tennis star Billie Jean King defeats Bobby Riggs at the Houston Astrodome in the "Battle of the Sexes." Billie Jean King became the first female athlete to earn more than $100,000.

1975   President Gerald R. Ford signs Public Law 95-106, authorizing women to enter the United States Military Academies for the first time. The same year, voters in Connecticut choose Ella T. Grasso as the first female governor in the United States elected in her own right.

1976   The ABC Evening News hires Barbara Walters as the first female national television news anchor.

1977   Janet Guthrie becomes the first woman driver to qualify for the Indianapolis 500.

1978   The State of Kansas elects Nancy Landon Kassebaum to the United States Senate, the first woman to serve in her own right.

1980   Sandra Day O'Connor is named the first female Justice on the United States Supreme Court.

1983   Sally Ride becomes the first American female astronaut.

1996   Madeline Albright becomes the first female Secretary of State.

2007   Nancy Pelosi becomes the first female Speaker of the House.

2007   The *New York Times* reports that 51 percent of American women now live without a husband.

2007   The Pew Research Center reports that since 1970, the number of American women who were better educated than their husbands increased from 20 to 28 percent; during the same period, the number of women who earned more money than their husband grew from 4 to 22 percent.

Historical Overview: The Roots of Radical Feminism

The era of the radical feminist is generally identified as the mid 1960s to the mid 1970s. Yet the roots of female radical activism reach deep into the nineteenth century and strike soil in the three traditional fields of progressive thought: The abolition and civil rights movement, women's suffrage movement, and the Far Left movement.

Abolition, Emancipation, Reconstruction, Civil Rights

The oldest model of an American progressive social movement for the radical feminist is seen in the revolt against slavery, and the subsequent push for emancipation and equal civil rights for African Americans. For the radical feminists, there were important similarities in the plights of African Americans and women in the United States. Each was an entire subpopulation systematically oppressed within the larger society. Although in many ways the bonds of slavery were more tactile and cruel, it involved only about 12 percent of the population in 1860.

At the same time, oppression of women affected a subculture which actually comprised 52 percent.

Long before the formal abolitionist movement began, slaves attempted revolts against their enslavers from the beginning, in active attempt to free themselves from bondage. One of greatest fears among the slave owners of the Deep South was a massive revolt of the slaves, overrunning the antebellum lifestyle and radically altering the balance of power. Whites in the South also harbored an irrational fear of black men relating sexually with white woman—while white men regularly had no compunction against having sex *and* procreating with black women. A further anxiety—which fueled the opposition against emancipation of the slaves—was the economic competition that would be created if two million slaves entered the free labor market—particularly en masse.

The most famous slave revolt in the United States involved a 31-year-old mystic and preacher named Nat Turner. In 1831, Turner had built a devoted following; he started a rampage through the plantations of Southampton, Virginia, with about 70 followers. Whites of Southampton fell into utter panic, but eventually Turner was tracked down, captured and executed.

A more successful revolt of slaves took place in 1793, 1,300 miles south across the Caribbean Sea in Saint-Domingue (now Haiti and the Dominican Republic). The rebellion was led by Toussaint L'ouverture, resulted in more than 60,000 deaths, but preceded the establishment of the independent republic of Haiti.

The year 1831 may be considered the beginning of the formal abolition movement, with the publication of the *The Liberator* (1831) by William Lloyd Garrison. *The Liberator* attracted contributors from throughout the young country, most notably sisters Sarah and Angelina Grimke. In 1836, Angelina Grimke contributed stirring words from her *An Appeal to Christian Women of the South:*

> . . . for if the women of the South do not rise in the strength of the Lord to plead with their fathers, brothers, and sons, that country must witness the most dreaded scenes of murder and blood. (Birney 1969, 140)

The work of the Grimke Sisters proved not only a seminal contribution to the abolition movement, but a critical inspiration for the slowly burgeoning women's movement as well.

In 1845, freed slave Frederick Douglass published his *Narrative of the Life of Frederick Douglass,* and began publishing the abolitionist newspaper, *North Star.* By 1848 he had become one of the nation's most distinguished abolitionist speakers and writers.

A pivotal moment in the abolition movement came in 1851, when a 40-year-old woman from Connecticut named Harriet Beecher Stowe wrote *Uncle Tom's Cabin.* The novel brought the plight of slavery to the American household. *Uncle Tom's Cabin* depicted the revolutionary work of the Underground Railroad, and heroic figures such as Harriet Tubman, who led slaves from the Deep South into the relative freedom of the North.

Following the onset of the Civil War in 1861, the passage of Emancipation Proclamation—which at the time might have been considered the culmination of the abolition movement—proved only to be the end of the beginning of the civil rights movement. With the passage of the 15th Amendment in 1869, many female abolitionists realized that many of the civil rights and opportunities they fought for on behalf of African Americans were being denied to women as well—including the suffrage the newly passed amendment procured. But through the Jim Crow period, the movement would seem to slumber for a time, but then would reawaken with explosiveness in the latter half of the twentieth century. It is partially out of the newly born civil rights movement that many of the radical feminists would emerge.

Women's Suffrage and Rights

The nineteenth century had its own version of radical feminists, whose primary goal became suffrage for women in the United States. Although hints of feminism appeared in such personages as Abigail Adams, Margaret Fuller, and Sojourner Truth, the first great forum for the advocacy of suffrage for women became the 1848 National Women's Rights Convention in Seneca Falls, New York. Organized by women such as Elizabeth Cady Stanton and Lucretia Mott, more than three hundred women and men—including abolition advocate Frederick Douglass—gathered in July in upstate New York. It was the first national women's rights convention in the United States, convened to address the prejudice of the male-dominated society, to launch the campaign for a new Constitutional amendment, which they hoped would ensure the right of the vote for women as well as blacks.

At the convention, Stanton presented her *Declarations of Rights and Sentiments,* modeled after Thomas Jefferson's Declaration of Independence. Before the gathered attendees, on July 19, Stanton fervently reflected the hopes of the assembled:

> We are assembled to protest against a form of government, existing without consent of the governed—to declare our right to be free as man is free, to be represented in the government which we are taxed to support, to have such disgraceful laws as to give man the power to chastise and imprison his wife, to take the wages which she earns, the property which she inherits and, in cases of separation, the children of her love ...
>
> The world has never seen a truly great and virtuous nation, because in the degradation of woman the very fountains of life are poisoned at their source. It is vain to look for silver and gold in mines of copper and lead. It is the wise mother that has the wise son. So long as your women are slaves, you may throw your colleges and churches to the winds ...
>
> To have drunkards, idiots, horse-racing, rum-selling rowdies, ignorant foreigners, and silly boys fully recognized, while we ourselves are thrust out from all rights that belong to citizens, it is too grossly insulting to the dignity of women to be longer quietly submitted to. The right is ours. Have it we must. Use it we will. The pens, the tongues, the fortunes, the indomitable wills of women are already pledged to secure that right. The great truth, that no just government can be formed without the consent of the governed, we shall echo and re-echo in the ears of the unjust judge until by continual coming we shall weary him ... (Miller 1995, 19)

Up until 1869, the abolitionism and women's suffrage shared more or less the same camps. But when a 15th Amendment was ratified in 1870, it ensured the vote for African American men, but not for women. At that point, the women's suffrage movement not only broke away from the abolitionist movement, but also it split into two factions. The American Women's Suffrage Association (AWSA), led by Lucy Stone, struck a mollifying stance toward women's suffrage. The AWSA platform did not stray too far from the traditional "women's sphere" of hearth and home. It took a patient stance on the 15th Amendment, conceding that the time for women would be another day. The AWSA focused on bringing about suffrage on a state-by-state level, as opposed to a more radical national constitutional amendment.

But the National Woman Suffrage Association (NWSA), led by Stanton and Susan B. Anthony, steered down a more radical route, proposing more sweeping social and political changes to improve status of women. Stanton, in particular, angered by what she saw as a betrayal by the abolitionists, became more aggressive and alienating in her speech and writings. The NWSA immediately advocated a constitutional amendment to guarantee women voting rights, and few men were admitted into their ranks. The NWSA provided a leftist lean to the AWSA's middle of the road approach, foreshadowing the emergence of radical and liberal feminism.

In the drive for the vote, women from across the country took radical steps in the direction of universal suffrage. In November of 1872, Susan B. Anthony herself was arrested for casting a vote for Ulysses S. Grant in Rochester, New York in the 1872 presidential election. During the course of her trial, Anthony gave her famous *On Women's Right to Vote* speech, in which she indicated:

> Webster, Worcester and Bouvier all define a citizen to be a person in the United States, entitled to vote and hold office. The only questions left to be settled now are: Are women persons? And I hardly believe any of our opponents will have the hardihood to say they are not. Being persons, then, women are citizens; and no state has a right to make any law, or to enforce any old law, that shall abridge their privileges and immunities (Linder 2006).

Meanwhile, one by one, suffrage was achieved in several of the western states, beginning with Wyoming Territory in 1869, which became a state in 1890. Wyoming was followed by Colorado (1893); Utah (1895); Idaho (1896); Washington (1910); California (1911); Oregon, Arizona, and Kansas (1912); Illinois (1913); Nevada and Montana (1914); and New York (1917). But still the nation lacked a federal ordinance, granting universal suffrage for women.

The original Radical Feminists: Susan B. Anthony and Elizabeth Cady Stanton. (Bettmann/CORBIS)

As the march towards universal suffrage continued, Elizabeth Cady Stanton continued down her own, more radical path. In 1895 she published *The Women's Bible*. An extremely radical effort for its time, *The Woman's Bible* shed light on how the *Bible* had been used for centuries as an instrument to justify the oppression of the women. *The Woman's Bible* presented the common Bible as a text written by men in ecclesiastical power, to keep women subordinate and ineffectual within the scope of the church:

> Others fear that they might compromise their evangelical faith by affiliating with those of more illiberal views, who do not regard the Bible as the Word of God, but like any other book, to be judged on its merits. If the Bible teaches the equality of Woman, why does the church refuse to ordain women to preach the gospel, to fill the offices of deacons and elders, to administer the Sacraments, or to admit them as delegates to the Synods, General Assemblies and Conferences of the different denominations?
>
> ... Why is it more ridiculous for women to protest against her present status in the Old and New Testament, in the ordinances and disciplines of the church, than in the statutes and constitutions of the state? Why is it more ridiculous to arraign ecclesiastics for their false teaching and acts of injustice to women, than members of Congress and the House of Commons? (Stanton 1974, 9–10).

All the while, pioneering women tested the limits of their rights and opportunities. Amelia Bloomer and Mary Walker dared to challenge the accepted mores of female fashion. Margaret Sanger championed the availability of birth control information and devices. Sarah Josepha Hale, Jennie June, Harriet Beecher Stowe, and Frances Whitaker blazed opportunities in the media. And women continually pushed against the patriarchal society's conventional definitions of "women's work": women such as Elizabeth Blackwell in medicine; Louise Blanchard Bethune in architecture; Frances E. Willard and Sophia Smith in higher education; Charlotte Ray and Belva Lockwood in law; Antoinette Blackwell and Mary Baker Eddy in ministry.

Finally in June 1919—72 years after the Seneca Falls Convention— the Susan B. Anthony Amendment was passed by the United States Senate by a vote of 66 to 30, sending the amendment on for ratification by the states. The ratification process would end August 18, 1920, as Tennessee became the 36th State to ratify the 19th Amendment to the U.S. Constitution. The tireless efforts by women's groups such as The National Women's Party, the National American Women's Suffrage Association, and the Congressional Union for Women's Suffrage paid off. On August 26, 1920, the 19th Amendment formally took effect: "The right of citizens of the United States to vote shall not be denied or abridged by the United States or by any state on account of sex."

Many have come to see the 19th Amendment as the end of the First Wave of Feminism in the United States. Like the Emancipation Proclamation, the Susan B. Anthony Amendment proved to be simply the end of the beginning in the fight for equal justice and opportunity. Some—like Alice Paul of the National Women's Party—immediately recognized that suffrage was not enough. In 1923, she wrote the Equal Rights Amendment, which would not be passed by Congress for another 49 years.

At the beginning of the twentieth century, the first wave of feminism finally gained a voice for women in the nation's so-called democratic process. By the end of the century the second wave—spearheaded by the radical feminists—would call for a revolutionary reworking of American culture, to give equal standing to women under law, and equal opportunity throughout society. Getting the vote, it was discovered, was not enough. Shulamith Firestone would later write:

> For what is the vote finally worth if the voter is manipulated? Every husband knows he's not losing a vote, but gaining one. Today, some fifty years later, women still vote as wives, just as they govern as wives (Firestone 1968, 7).

The radical feminists wanted women to vote as women, and to govern as women—not as agents to their spouses.

The American Radical Left and Labor Movements

Both the abolition/reconstruction movement and the Suffrage movement sought to reform the nineteenth century American system to include both African Americans and women in the electoral process. But it became abundantly clear that simply having the right to vote did not confer equal rights, standing, and opportunities under the law and in the marketplace.

In the meantime, there was a growing segment of the population that wanted not simply to reform the current system, but replace it with forms of democratic capitalism and socialism. This was the Far Left movement, which modeled the radical for the radical feminist. (Many radical feminists—including Jane Alpert, Rosalyn Baxandall, Dana Densmore, Roxanne Dunbar, Kathie Sarachild, and Barbara Winslow—had relatives or parents who were active on the Left side of the political persuasion).

By the end of the Civil War, the industrial revolution had come to the United States in full bloom. Many laborers found themselves at the mercy of the industrial capitalists, with few protections against exploitations, and no share in the distribution of wealth and power. At the same time, the writings of Karl Marx and Frederick Engels began to infiltrate the consciousness of the American worker. Journals such as *Woodhull & Claflin Weekly*—published by Victoria Woodhull, who ran for President on the Equal Rights Party in 1872—released copies of *Das Kapital* for the American proletariat to read. Marx argued that the "full realization of the principle of equivalent exchange is no more than a step toward genuine equality, liberty, and fraternity ..." (Clecak 1973, 22). American workers became motivated by these words.

The ideals of the Far Left emerged within the labor movements of the latter 19th century. Workers realized they would have to band together if they were to counterbalance the oppression of the industrial elite. Phrases such as Marx's "from each according to his ability, to each according to his needs" and "philosophers only interpret the world; the proletariat can change it" began to take root in some laborers' consciousness. Efforts of the Far Left sought to raise the downtrodden proletariat through revolutionary action to change the structure, not just the liberal reform of the already existing oppressive structure. Communism sought to democratize economic and political power in a no-class society

One by one, groups of workers unionized—overcoming differences in language, culture, and personal perception—to use the power of the collective workforce to gain rights, protection, and compensation. Between 1881 and 1906, more than 30 thousand strikes affecting more than nine million workers sprang up throughout the country.

In 1860, 10 thousand shoe workers in Lynn, Massachusetts, organized a strike to gain wages. In the 1870s, the Irish Coal mine workers—known as the Molly Maguires—went on strike against the horrendous conditions and paltry wages offered by the mine owners. In 1869, the Knights of Labor—the forerunners to the American Federation of Labor—formed to unionize railroad workers facing low pay and unreasonable hours. In 1894, the American Railroad Union was organized under Eugene Debs to strike against the Pullman Car Company. The walkout included more than 60 thousand workers, affecting railroad operation throughout the nation. In 1886, the American Federation of Labor—under president Samuel Gompers—organized skilled workers throughout the country to win advances in wages, work hours, employer liability, work safety, and the rights of collective bargaining. Finally in 1905, the Industrial Workers of the World—known as The Wobblies—was formed, eventually drawing a standing membership of more than 100 thousand workers.

Meanwhile farmers, particularly in the south and the west, faced increasing oppression from banks and manufacturers. In 1892, they organized the People's, or Populist, Party, which sought to transfer power held by industrial conglomerates to the people. Among the ideas of the Populist Party were such socialist notions as national ownership of railroads, telephone and telegraph systems, and a graduated income tax.

At the turn of the twentieth century a growing literate segment of the population became known as "Lyrical Left", as socialism managed to develop into an affecting political force. The growth of socialism came from an absorption of populist ideas, spurred on by waves of European immigration, which heightened the prestige of European socialists. In 1920, Eugene Debs represented the Socialist Democratic Party in a run for President of the United States. Debs gained nearly one million votes in what became the pinnacle of influence for socialism in the United States.

At the same time, the anarchists—who sought to replace government with free cooperation among individuals—made their imprint on American society. Perhaps the most famous American anarchist was Emma Goldman, who might have been a prototype for the radical feminists 60 years later. Born in 1867 in Lithuania to the home of a volatile and abusive father, Emma immigrated to Rochester,

New York. She became inspired by the growing anarchism movement, fueled by the 1886 Haymakers Strike in Chicago. By age 20, she was a full-fledged revolutionary, often advocating anarchic social positions and the use of violence to bring them about. As an early radical feminist, Emma Goldman sought to transform the institutions of marriage, abolish economic dependency, and purge society of prostitution and venereal disease. She also understood that suffrage alone would never truly liberate women. In her lectures Goldman presented a truly prophetic concept:

> The right to vote, or equal civil rights, may be good demands, but true emancipation begins neither at the polls nor in courts. It begins in woman's soul. History tells us that every oppressed class gained true liberation from its masters through its own efforts. It is necessary that woman learn that lesson, that she may realize that her freedom will reach as far as her power to achieve her freedom reaches. It is, therefore, far more important for her to begin with her inner regeneration, to cut loose from the weight of prejudices, traditions, and customs. The demand for equal rights in every vocation of life is just and fair; but, after all, the most vital right is the right to love and be loved. Indeed if partial emancipation is to become a complete and true emancipation of women, it will have to do away with the ridiculous notion that to be loved, to be sweetheart and mother, is synonymous with being a slave or subordinate. It will have to do away with the absurd notion of the dualism of the sexes, or that a man and woman represent two antagonistic worlds (Shulman, 1972, 142).

By the time of her death in 1940, "Red Emma" came to personify the archetype indefatigable radical. In 1892, she had become close friends with anarchist Alexander Berkman, who shot Henry Clay Frick during the strike at the Homestead plant of Carnegie Steel in 1892. She was imprisoned in 1893 at Blackwell Prison for inciting unemployed workers to steal bread. In 1901 she was linked with fellow anarchist Leon Czolgosz, and arrested in Chicago on charges—which were eventually cleared—of conspiracy to assassinate President William McKinley. In 1916, she was imprisoned for advertising and distributing birth control literature through her radical feminist journal, *Mother Earth*. She found herself behind prison walls again in 1917, for conspiring to obstruct military conscription. After the Justice Department raided the *Mother Earth* offices, she was deported to Russia in 1919, in time to witness the repercussions of the Bolshevik Revolution. In 1936, she traveled to Spain to support the Spanish Republic's fight against fascist Francisco Franco. Never once did she seem to sway from her anarchic ties or beliefs. And after she died of a stroke in Toronto, Canada, in 1940, her tombstone read: "Liberty will not descend to the people, a people must raise themselves to Liberty."

The advent of World War I created a fissure between nationalism and socialism. The war became linked to imperialism by socialists, and in turn, many socialists and communists were persecuted. The Lyrical Left became curtailed by the Red Scare and antisedition legislation under Wilson, such as the Espionage Act of 1917, which, for example, denied the Socialist Democratic Party postal privileges. With the close of World War I, America seemed to withdraw to nurse its wounds from the brutal global conflict with salves of materialism, hedonism, and celebration. The nation turned away from any leftist ideas of restructuring American society, preferring to concentrate on the indulgences and frivolity of a nation recovering from a brutal war. The apathy of the 20s constricted idealistic thought of the Lyrical Left. But the party atmosphere of the 1920s eventually gave way to the stark realism of the great depression.

The movement which would become characterized as the "Old Left" emerged in the 1930s in response to the "failure of capitalism" during the Depression. Although efforts arose to resurrect the socialistic ideas of pre–World War I, the working class in America remained largely conservative, essentially blaming itself for its predicament, rather than the inequality of the class structure. The New Deal rose above the interests of the ruling class, responding to the needs of organized labor and the majority of citizens. Meanwhile, the country—faced with the reported horrors of Joseph Stalin's perverted Soviet version of socialism—curtailed the emergence of the Left in the United States. Although Stalin poisoned the socialist experiment, the United States was already engaged in such socialist programs such as welfare, labor relations, and mass education. The industrial push of World War II saved the American economy, and quickly consumerism and materialism attracted the attention of the American populace—much as had happened after World War I.

The American worker did not experience the "increasing misery" of the old world laborer. For the American workers, consumer materialism remained a goal, and the capitalist system provided enough relative abundance for the majority of the populace to keep them from seeking alternative systems of government and finance. The seeds of revolution never got a chance to germinate. The role of the far left remained to push the liberal element towards reform in areas otherwise unexplored. European ideology was seen as leading to fascism and totalitarianism, which made capitalistic America look good in the 40s and 50s. Yet the Left provided heroes that could be emulated in progressive movements in the future. These included Big Bill Haywood, proletariat poet and feared American radical. As one time head of the World Federation of Miners, and then the International Workers of the World, Haywood was captured and jailed in 1905 by Pinkerton detectives in connection with the Colorado Labor Wars. John Silas Reed was a journalist renowned for his account of the Bolshevik revolution in Russia in *Ten Days That Shook the World*. He became known as the "Patron Saint of the American Communist Party." There was Victor Berger, who in 1910 became the first socialist to serve in Congress; Daniel Deleon, the "metaphysician of socialism" and the foremost American thinker on industrial unionism; and Max Eastman, progressive Harlem renaissance writer and editor of *The Masses*. Socialism rekindled interest in the writings of Henry David Thoreau, instigated fascination for the stories of Jack London, and Charlotte Perkins Gilman, who brought a women's point of view to American economics.

The New Left: 1956–1970

The economic affluence and government expansion of the post–World War II era planted the seeds of political disillusionment and the assumption of powerlessness among the younger generation, often called the "Ungeneration." The nation wanted a "breather" from the hectic 1930s and 1940s, and the populace turned to suburbanism and consumerism to buffer itself from the realities of the cold war. Opportunities for ethnic groups and women that had sprung up during the war dried up as the servicemen returned to the United States, and competition for employment intensified. Any anti-American demonstrations were quickly curtailed by the allegations of McCarthyism. But during this period of apathy two issues infiltrated the nation's consciousness: racial discrimination and nuclear disarmament

Out of the cultural disillusion and alienation came a New Left movement, not so much concerned about the working class or proletariat—as the Old or Lyrical Left was—but about the disenfranchised. In 1959 Fidel Castro's Communist Party came into power in Cuba, and Castro was seen as a new breed of radical. The emerging New Left rejected the idea of Cuba as communist conspiracy in the Western Hemisphere but saw instead a lone revolution by a poor country against the autocratic ruler Fulgencio Batista. Combined with the 1960 election of John Fitzgerald Kennedy as President, Castro and Kennedy became symbols of the potency and potential of a young generation, with fresh ideas and energy.

In the meantime, the civil rights movement had begun in the South. Martin Luther King Jr. had organized the Montgomery Bus Boycott in 1954, to protest the segregation of the city's public transit lines. In February 1960, the first sit-in at the Woolworth Counter in Greensboro, North Carolina, was organized by the Student Non-Violent Coordinating Committee (SNCC), which also spearheaded the Freedom Rides and black voter registration drives in the Deep South. The SNCC became the shock troop of civil rights movement. It recruited and sent eight hundred white students from the North to help with voter registration in the South. It also became the first civil rights group to oppose the war in Vietnam.

The SNCC influenced the 1964 Civil Rights Law, the 1965 Voting Rights Law, and the Johnson Administration's War on Poverty. It became a model for another prominent New Left organization, the Students for a Democratic Society (SDS), with its participatory democracy and parallel structures. Organizations such as SDS did not want to repair and reform the current society, but develop a new society in which Marxist ideas of socialism replaced what was the oppressive practices of capitalism. They were anti-anti-communists, who tried to ignite an interracial movement of poor. It developed the

Economic Research and Action Project (ERAP), as SDS initiated a university-backed program of economic and social reforms within the communities of the most impoverished.

In May of 1963, SDS issued its Port Huron Statement in Ann Arbor, Michigan. The document, written by future California State Senator Tom Hayden, criticized the American military industrial complex, advocating converting military money into social programs. It criticized the American public for being lulled into complacency due to consumerism, and depending so much on military spending for its prosperity. It also condemned the entrance of the United States into the war in Vietnam.

Other events stirred the unrest of the Ungeneration. In 1960, the execution of Caryl Chessman sparked a drive to ban the death penalty in California, and caused the questioning of the validity of all laws. In the same year, the San Francisco hearings and subsequent student protests of the House Un-American Activities Committee (HUAC) was captured in a film by the committee *Operation Abolition,* and shown in college campuses across the country. The film—which sought to support the HUAC—backfired, sparking opposition among college students, and inadvertently supporting the activist culture. In 1964, Mario Salvo's Free Speech Movement emerged at University of California at Berkeley, where the student body protested the suppression of political and social information for its edification. And in 1965, the SDS organized the first national demonstration against Vietnam, as 25 thousand marchers converged on Washington in April of that year.

As time went on, many in the civil rights movement abandoned the goal of integration, disillusioned with the goal when it was discovered that many of the whites involved in the movement did not necessarily hold the best interests of African Americans. Many felt the nonviolence of King was only preached because the blacks would be outnumbered and legally outmaneuvered by whites if violence broke out. Many African Americans rejected King's goal of nonviolent integration for the more aggressive stance of Black Power advocated by Malcolm X. The New Left movement became fractured between factions of black and white.

Among the volunteers drawn by the SNCC and other organizations were scores of young female college students. These intrepid women traveled to the South to aid in the SNCC registration of African American voters, and to participate in the Freedom Rides of the Congress of Racial Equality (CORE). They flocked to groups such as SDS and the Radical Youth Movement, determined to work side by side with men to overturn an oppressive and imperialistic regime, and to campaign for the end of the war. Many women learned the radical techniques developed under SNCC or SDS.

Yet as these women watched African Americans struggle to alleviate their own disenfranchisement, they grew painfully aware of the discrimination and oppression they experienced as a gender. They became tired of the white males of the New Left movement relegating women to second-class status and responsibilities. But when women criticized accepted sex roles, and advocated for societal changes benefiting women—such as communal child care, accessible abortions, birth control information, sharing housework—they were belittled and muffled by the elites in the movement. Many of these women began to realize that the same oppressive societal structures which held down the blacks in the form of racism also restricted the opportunities for women in the form of sexism. Before long, the New Left movement would not only be split along ethic lines but along gender lines as well. The lessons of the nineteenth century suffragists and abolitionists would have to be learned one more time.

The tenets of radical feminism began to emerge out of the early stages of the New Left movement in America: "The women's liberation movement was generated by women within SDS who rebelled against 'male supremacy' in that organization and in the New Left movement as a whole" (Diggins 1992, 233).

Although SDS and SNCC headed the list of New Left organizations, there were plenty of other causes to draw the disillusioned young adult. The list included the RYM (Revolutionary Youth Movement I) also known as the Weathermen. Taking their title from the lyrics of Bob Dylan's "Subterranean Homesick Blues," the Weathermen engaged in what they saw as heroic action designed to bring the system to its knees. The Weathermen felt the blacks couldn't do it alone, and so the whites should support black efforts to fight racism. But by 1970 the Weatherman had failed to gain the sympathies of most Americans. It headed underground, and added to the violence of the movement under the label of "revolution," which contributed to the eventual demise of the New Left as an organized movement.

Other prominent New Left groups included the Youth International Party Yippies, of Abbie Hoffman and Jerry Rubin fame, and the Black Panther Party (BPP) led by Huey Newton and Bobby Seale. The BPP became known for their heroic action—particularly early on—as they identified the enemy as the white ruling class, and not just the average "whitey." There were also Dave Dellinger's MOBE (Mobilization Committee to End the War in Vietnam), and the SWP (Socialist Workers Party).

These New Left organizations all shared a common heritage in their treatment of women within their ranks, a heritage which seemed to reflect the society at large. Ironically the men in the organization seemed to be so committed to changing the ways that oppressed the general society. Yet they still clung to the sexist notions that— consciously or unconsciously—supported the oppression of women.

Works Cited

Birney, Catherine H., *The Grimke Sisters: Sarah and Angelina Grimke*, Westport, CT: Greenwood Press Publishers, 1969, 140.

Clecak, Peter, *Radical Paradoxes*, New York: Harper & Row Publishers, 1973, 22.

Diggins, John Patrick, *The Rise and Fall of the American Left*, New York: W. W. Norton & Company, 1992, 233.

Firestone, Shulameth, "The Women's Rights Movement in America," *Notes from the First Year*, New York Radical Women, 1968, 7.

Linder, Douglas, "Susan B. Anthony: A Biography," http://www.law.umkc.edu/ faculty/projects/ftrials/anthony/defargument.html.

Miller, Bradford, *Returning to Seneca Falls*, Hudson, NY: Lindsfarne Press, 1995, 19.

Shulman, Alix Kates, ed., *Red Emma Speaks: Selected Writings and Speeches*, New York: Vintage, 1972, 142.

Stanton, Elizabeth Cady, "Preface," *The Women's Bible*, Coalition Task Force on Women and Religion, 1974, 9–10.

| # Publications, Documents, and Manifestoes

Two Early Influential Books

Between 1949 and 1963, two important literary works emerged in the Western world, awakening a realization within women about themselves, their social and political status, and the potential for major change in the United States and around the world. These books set the tone for the approaching women's movement, and helped develop the imaginations of the radical feminists.

Simone de Beauvoir's *The Second Sex*, (1949)

The first was written by Simone de Beauvoir, the 41-year-old companion of French philosopher Jean-Paul Sarte. Called the *The Second Sex (Le Deuxieme Sexe)*, it was a landmark text, casting Beauvoir in the role of mother of modern feminism. *The Second Sex* provided a theoretical tool for the women's movement, which picked up on themes developed in the book: the denunciation of cultural myths; the questioning of marriage, the family, and motherhood; the boredom of housewives; the economic dependence of married women; the multiple taboos surrounding women's sex lives and their lack of

Simone De Beauvoir, author of The Second Sex. *(Hulton-Deutsch Collection/CORBIS)*

freedom. *The Second Sex* brought all of these ideas to be examined side by side in one volume.

Simone de Beauvoir was a Marxist who believed the overthrow of capitalism would bring about the liberation of women and make them men's equals. For Beauvoir, it was not a question of women finding a place in society as it was, but transforming society itself. She not only demanded an improvement in women's conditions but also questioned the continued existence of the very system that engendered inequalities and injustice.

When her book came out in 1949, Beauvoir came under heavy criticism in France, a patriarchal country where suffrage had not even arrived until 1947. Beauvoir's critics accused her of misogyny—even if unconscious—and of devaluing the feminine difference, repressed under patriarchy.

However, her many supporters praised *The Second Sex* as a window through which women could finally look at their own situation. In *The Making of an Intellectual Woman*, writer Toril Moi said, "Beauvoir provided women all over the world with a vision of change" (Moi 1994, 24). British Scholar Terry Keefe called it "one of the most important and far-reaching books on women ever published" (Bair 1990, 388). More important, it became formative reading for many of the major figures in the radical feminist movement, such as Rosalyn Baxandall, Dana Densmore, Mary Daly, and more. Many of the radical ideas proposed in feminist literature were first suggested in the pages of *The Second Sex*.

In *The Second Sex*, Beauvoir examined with a skeptical, discerning eye the female experience from varying aspects. She challenged the myths of pregnancy and questioned the influence of biology on the oppressed position of women. She rebelliously characterized gestation as "a fatiguing task of no individual benefit to the woman, but on the contrary demanding heavy sacrifices" (DeBeauvoir 1989, 30). She questioned the alleged divine inspiration for the subordination of women, writing biological factors "are insufficient for setting up a hierarchy of the sexes; they fail to explain why the woman is the 'Other'" (DeBeauvoir 1989, 33).

She suggested that marriage was a kind of servitude traditionally, and noted that marriage and prostitution seemed to appear hand in hand in society. She also wrote that lesbians seemed to offer an alternate path, separate from the dominance of men. She acknowledged women as economic competition for men, but questioned the character of men who were threatened by women in the workplace, writing, "No one is more arrogant toward women, more aggressive or scornful, than the man who is anxious about his virility" (DeBeauvoir 1989, xxxi). And she asserted that it was difficult to judge the appropriateness of women in the workplace without giving them an adequate opportunity: "What gives rise to much of the debate is the tendency to reduce her to what she has been, to what she is today, in raising the question of her capabilities; for the fact is that capabilities are clearly manifested only when they have been realized ... domestic labors that fell to her lot because they were reconcilable with the cares of maternity imprisoned her in repetition and immanence" (DeBeauvoir 1989, 63). She believed that it was woman's economic dependence on men which created the second-class position, and said that until women were accorded the same opportunities as men, they would remain in that position: "Civil liberties remain theoretical as long as they are unaccompanied by economic freedom ... she remains bound to her condition of vassalage" (DeBeauvoir 1989, 679). She also recognized that the patriarchal family favored private property, and that private property marked the beginning of the downturn from matriarchy to patriarchy. She equated paternalism with capitalism, thus launching the theme for the politicos of the women's movement, which also rang the death knell for capitalism. She also identified the penchant the capitalistic/paternalistic system had for war, stating "superiority has been accorded in humanity not to the sex that brings forth but to that which kills" (DeBeauvoir 1989, 64). Beauvoir also challenged many of the myths that had developed around woman, particularly under the label of Freudian thought. She suggested that penis envy may have more to do with the privileges men enjoy over women than the anatomical construction. She also noted the problem of trying to explain female sexuality when psychoanalysts at the time were all male.

Ultimately, Beauvoir made the point that men were considered more than their biology, and women were not. She stated the matter plainly to a 1949 readership:

"Yes, women on the whole *are* inferior to men; that is, their situation affords them fewer possibilities. The question is: should that state of affairs continue?" (DeBeauvoir 1989, xxx). The response by the radical feminists would be a resounding "No!"

Betty Friedan's *The Feminine Mystique*, (1963)

The second book that greatly influenced the radical feminist movement was released by publisher W. W. Norton and Company in 1963. *The Feminine Mystique*, by Betty Friedan, articulated particularly for millions of American women that there was more to life than raising children and running a household. In it, Friedan wrote:

Why have so many American wives suffered the nameless aching dissatisfaction for so many years, each one thinking she was alone ... ? A Houston, Texas, housewife wrote: "It has been the feeling of being almost alone with my problem that has made it so hard. I thank God for my family, home and the chance to take care of them, but my life couldn't stop there. It is an awakening to know that I'm not an oddity and can stop being ashamed of wanting more" (Friedan 1963, 33).

The book hit a nerve with women who identified with the civil rights movement, because they themselves had lived lives of limited opportunity. Regarded as one of the most influential books of the twentieth century, *The Feminine Mystique* would sell more than three million copies by the year 2000, translated into many foreign languages. Like *The Second Sex*, it found its way into the hands of many of the women who would campaign for rights and opportunities for women in the years to come.

Friedan, a 33-year-old editor from Peoria, Illinois, had been educated at UC Berkeley, studying under famed child psychologist Erik Erikson. She reportedly grew up brainy, ungainly, and outspoken. Friedan's often blunt persona continued after the book made her world famous. *The Feminine Mystique* anointed Betty Friedan as one of the chief players in the modern women's movement. She would go forward to help found the National Organization for Women (NOW), remaining as its president from 1966 to 1970. She would also become a point of contention for the radical feminists, as she tried to steer the women's movement down the Main Street of middle America. She died in 2006.

The First Manifesto: "Sex and Caste: A Kind of Memo"

The first rumblings of the movement to liberate women within the radical Left could be heard in November of 1964, at a retreat to evaluate the Student Nonviolent Coordinating Committee (SNCC) in Waveland, Mississippi. It was here that Stokely Carmichael (the would-be executive chairman of the SNCC), was asked the question, "What is the position of women in the SNCC?" His answer has become infamous: "The position of women in the SNCC is prone!" (Echols 1989, 31). In truth Carmichael gave a candid if highly insensitive assessment of the role that women seemed expected to play within the New Left. The needs of women were trivialized, and most women were relegated to "women's work," providing clerical support for the organizations, and physical and emotional comfort for the men.

A popular slogan during the antiwar movement was, "Girls say yes to men who say no." Men in the New Left seemed to resist and deny the existence of sexual inequality more than racial inequality. Neither the SNCC nor the Students for a Democratic Society (SDS) wanted to challenge the sexual injustice inherent in the organizations, and there was little to no acknowledgement of women's issues. Sexual inequality was rampant in the Summer of Freedom, which blatantly revealed the disparity of roles for women in the project. Just as suffrage for blacks enflamed the movement for women in the nineteenth century, civil rights work for blacks enflamed civil rights work for women in the twentieth.

Out of the SNCC retreat appeared a document written on the position of women in the movement. Originally attributed to Ruby Doris Smith Robinson, it was actually written by civil rights workers Mary King and Casey Hayden, wife of Tom Hayden (who wrote the SDS Port Huron Manifesto in 1962). The women wanted to write something about the status of women in the SNCC using civil rights type terminology:

> The average white person finds it difficult to understand why the Negro resents being called "boy" or being thought of as "musical" or "athletic" because the average white person doesn't realize that he assumes he is superior. And naturally he doesn't understand the problem of paternalism. So too the average SNCC worker finds it difficult to discuss the women problem because of the assumption of male superiority. Assumptions of male superiority are as wide-spread and deep rooted and every much as crippling to the woman as the assumptions of white supremacy are to the Negro (Berkeley 1999, 41).

Cowriter Mary King later talked about how she wrote the essay with trepidation that it would not be taken seriously. As the women feared, their position paper was roundly criticized during its formal presentation and became the butt of Carmichael's joke.

The following year, at the SDS National Council meeting in Champaign-Urbana, Illinois, in December of 1965, King and Hayden released the document in the form of a manifesto. "Sex and Caste: A Kind of Memo" was introduced at the SDS workshop on Women's

Roles, and was published in the April 1966 edition of *Liberation* magazine. Reportedly Mary King wrote it, and Casey Hayden signed on to give it added support. When King presented it orally at the workshop, reportedly few people agreed with her. Little did she know of the energy her words would spark, or the enthusiastic responses they would engender for years to come:

> Many people who are very hip to the implications of the racial caste system, even people in the movement, don't seem to be able to see the sexual caste system . . . At the same time, very few men can respond non-defensively, since the whole idea is either beyond their comprehension or threatens them or exposes them (King and Hayden 1966, 47).

Women organized a workshop to separate them from the defensiveness the men of the Left exhibited over the issue of sexual inequality. But while "Sex and Caste" seemed to be a hit among the white women of the movement, black women did not respond to the manifesto, seemingly holding the idea that racial discrimination was the bigger issue, with sexual discrimination a secondary concern.

Essentially, the SDS became a microcosm for the oppression of women in society at large. Women faced the same challenges within an organization committed to freedom. Women wanted equality in a just society, because equality in an unjust society is meaningless. Meanwhile, men in organizations became threatened by the women's demands. Radical men grew more hostile toward women, as the white man slowly found himself exiled from both the racial and sexual movements.

Despite the oppression they found within these organizations, the women learned community organizing, which would be put to work in organizing the women's liberation movement. The skills valued in community organizing—warmth, empathy, noncompetitiveness— had already been encouraged in women traditionally, and soon they would be used for the advantage of radical women.

"Toward a Female Liberation Movement"

In 1968, the first women's liberation group from the South released a monumental document. Entitled "Toward a Female Liberation Movement" (Addendum 1), it became known as "The Florida Paper" because it was released by Gainesville Women's Liberation, centered at the University of Florida in Gainesville. Gainesville was regarded as the "Berkeley of the South," while Gainesville Women's Liberation, founded by Carol Giardina, had emerged as one of the first five women's liberation groups in the country.

Verbalizing the sentiments of radical women from around the country, the Florida Paper was written by Judith Brown and Beverly Jones, who had met at the University of Florida at a demonstration of the students' civil rights organization. The document became widely regarded as the first theoretical framework for the women's movement. In it, Jones and Brown advocated separation by women from the men in the New Left Movement. It criticized the failing leadership of men in the movement, stating, "One of the serious flaws in most radical male thinking is the substitution of goals for tactics" (Jones and Brown 1968, 25).

The paper described the oppressive nature of the New Left Movement from the female point of view. It advocated for the creation of all-female communes, where women could hopefully experience a break from the dominant-submissive status quo of the nuclear family. The paper also encouraged women to examine the possibilities of celibacy and lesbianism as alternatives, without succumbing to the disparaging hostility of men toward female homosexuality.

"Toward a Female Liberation Movement" was met with such resistance locally from men and businesses that Gainesville Women's Liberation had to resort to distributing it in women's restrooms. But women such as Naomi Weisstein, then active with the Chicago Women's Liberation Movement, commented:

> It transformed our thinking, and we were ecstatic over it. Now we knew we were doing the right thing. Here was a vision of the liberation of women so real, so palpable and compelling that our doubts dissolved ... After that paper, there would be no turning back for us, or the rest of the movement (Brown 1998, 1).

Author Judith Brown had enrolled in the University of Florida Master's Program in English, and graduated from the university's law school. In 1963, she worked as a CORE (Congress of Racial Equality) organizer in Gadsen County, Florida, and was arrested several times in protests against segregation. She eventually became a partner with Albert Bacharach in the law firm Brown & Bacharach, and would die in 1991 due to breast cancer. The Judith Brown Women's Liberation Leadership Endowment Scholarship was formed at the Center for Women's Studies and Gender Research in her honor. Coauthor Beverly Jones had helped found the Gainesville Women for Equal Rights, which worked to end segregation in work sites. Jones eventually went to work for NOW.

Using language of the civil rights movement, for which both Jones and Brown had worked, Jones wrote in the first half of the document:

> There is almost an exact parallel between the role of women and the role of black people in this society. Together they constitute the great maintenance force sustaining the white American Male. They wipe his ass and breast feed him when he is little, they school him in his youthful years, do his clerical work and raise his and their replacements later, and all throughout his life in the factories, on the migrant farms, in the restaurants, hospitals, offices, and homes, they sew for him, stoop for him, cook for him, clean for him, sweep, run errands, haul away his garbage, and nurse him when his frail body falters ...
>
> Let's get together to decide in groups of women how to get out of this bind, to discover and fight the techniques of domination in and out of the home ... to change our physical and social surroundings, to free our time, our energy, and our minds, to start to build for ourselves, for all mankind, a world without horrors (Jones and Brown 1968, 4).

Brown continued the call for a separate campaign for women in the second half of the paper, asserting that:

> Yet we, like radical men, have only one life we know of. It is a serious question whether we should live it as slaves to the rhetoric, the analysis, and the discipline of the movement we have come to be a part of, if that movement, that analysis, and that discipline systematically deprive us of our pride, genuine relationships with free women, equal relationships with men, and a sense that we are using our talents and dedication to a committed life as fully and as freely as possible (Jones and Brown 1968, 19).

The First Newsletter: *Notes from the First Year*

Also in 1968, the New York Radical Women released its classic newsletter, entitled *Notes from the First Year*, which would be subsequently followed by *Notes from the Second Year* and *Notes from the Third Year*. Compared favorably to the nineteenth century *Revolution*, released by Elizabeth Cady Stanton and Susan B. Anthony, articles featured essays on women's sexuality, abortion, the women's rights movement, and women in the radical movement, written by such luminaries as Katie Amatniek (Sarachild), Rosalyn Baxandall, Cindy Cisler, Shulamith Firestone, Carol Hanisch, and Anne Koedt.

A Woman's Psychology: Naomi Weisstein's "Kinder, Kirche, Kuche"

That year brought about several advances in feminist tenets, including the importance of consciousness-raising and attitudes toward sex. In further support of the feminist faction, under the assertion that modern psychology has no idea about the female personality or "the clinical nature of women," Naomi Weisstein released "Kinder, Kuche, Kirche as Scientific Law: Psychology Constructs the Female (or the Fantasy Life of the Male Psychologist)" (Addendum 3). This first edition was published by New England Free Press in Boston, but would be released a total of 42 times in six languages.

In her groundbreaking paper, Weisstein challenged the views held by most male psychologists—and therefore, at the time, most psychologists—which reflected the cultural consensus: that a woman is defined by her ability to attract men, and her life's task is one of "joyful altruism and nurturance." Weisstein asserted that psychology has nothing to say about what women want, need, or like, because the psychology of women was not known. She contradicted the assumption that human behavior rests on an individual and inner dynamic and criticized such a position without looking at the social context.

Weisstein asserted that the assumptions psychology made about women were based on theory without evidence. She suggested that "years of intensive, clinical experience" (i.e., what Sigmund Freud had produced) were not the same as empirical evidence. She proclaimed there indeed was no evidence of the ability to judge between "male behavior" v. "female behavior" or, for that matter, heterosexual v. homosexual behavior. She wrote that groups behave very often the way they are expected to behave, and that the study of behavior requires the study of social context: "Psychologists must realize that it is they who are limiting discovery of human potential ... it is clear that until social expectations for men and women are equal, until we provide equal respect for both men and women, our answers to these questions will simply reflect our prejudices" (Weisstein 1968, 10).

Weisstein would go on to advocate for the idea of social construction, which she defined as "an understanding among mainstream psychologists of how important social context is in determining behavior" (Weisstein 1997, 2).

Pregnancy, Childbirth, and Family: Shulamith Firestone's *The Dialectic of Sex*

In 1970 several important pieces of radical feminist literature came to be published. Shulamith Firestone published *The Dialectic of Sex* in October of 1970. In this radical, futuristic book, Firestone synthesizes ideas of Sigmund Freud, Karl Marx, Wilhelm Reich, and Frederick Engels—including the dialectic technique of analysis—with radical feminism. Firestone argues that the oppressed position was forced on women due to biology. Pregnancy, childbirth, and subsequent child rearing made them ultimately dependent on males. She described pregnancy as barbaric, compared it to defecating a pumpkin, and advocated for the scientific alleviation of that the role. Firestone foresaw human reproduction through laboratories and artificial wombs, predicting sex selection and in vitro fertilization.

She advocated unrestricted access to contraception and government-sponsored child care and advocated the abolition of nuclear family, seen as the nucleus of the tyranny against women. Instead, she suggested the development of community units within socialistic society, where children would be raised insulated from the sexist and repressive modes of family life. She said sexual repression to keep nuclear family intact creates neurosis and cultural illness. Firestone not only traced the development of economic classes to organic causes, but linked sexual oppression to the heart of economic oppression: "Marx was onto something more profound than he knew when he observed that the family contained within itself in miniature all the antagonisms that later develop on a wide scale in the society and the state" (Firestone 1970, 12). She wrote that the socialist movement was shortsighted in that it looked at economics only, and not the oppression of the family structure.

In her futuristic vision, Firestone proposed an alternate system, which featured freedom from the tyranny of reproductive biology. She campaigned for full self-determination—including economic— for women and children, and the total integration of women and children into larger society, which operates out of feminist socialism rather than wages. She also advocated for freedom of sexuality for women and children, and envisioned the intimacy and support provided by community child rearing, where children have an opportunity to be raised by a number of points of view.

Sex and Love Are Different Things: Pam Kearnon's "Man-Hating"

Also in 1970, Pam Kearnon published her essay, "Man-Hating," in the New York Radical Women's *Notes from the Second Year*. In it she told her readers that sex and love are not the same, and that men could and would have sex with women while actually hating them. She wrote that people do not react to oppression with love. She further stated that man-hating creates a deep rift within women's movement, which she challenged to direct the anger toward the oppressor, and not the victim.

Success and Power: Jo Freeman's "The Bitch Manifesto"

Meanwhile Jo Freeman, under the pen name Joreen, published one of the most creative and provocative essays of the era, "The BITCH Manifesto" (Addendum 4).

She takes the term "bitch," a commonly used derogative for an assertive female, and turns it around to create a virtual badge of courage for the feminist movement.

Freeman writes that the word is used to describe women who "rudely violate conceptions of proper sex role behavior." She asserts that bitches are androgynous, wanting to be identified as human as well as female—in fact, insist on being human first. The essay invites women to embrace the term as an indication of success; a woman is breaking out of the demure, dependent, and submissive role society had carved out for her. This is, in short, the essential goal of the women's liberation movement.

> Our society has defined humanity as male, and female as something other than male. In this way, females could be human only by living vicariously through a male. To be able to live, a woman has to agree to serve, honor, and obey a man and what she gets in exchange is at best a shadow of a life. Bitches refuse to serve, honor, and obey anyone. They demand to be fully functional human beings, not just shadows (Brown, 1997).

"The BITCH Manifesto" resounded through Women's Movement, because so many members no doubt had become quite familiar with the term in a personal way. Freeman urged "a woman should be proud to declare she is a Bitch, because Bitch is Beautiful."

Sex Is Political: Kate Millett's *Sexual Politics*

Finally, in 1970, Kate Millett released *Sexual Politics: A Manifesto for Revolution*, which had started out as her master's thesis at Columbia University.

In *Sexual Politics*, Millett criticized a patriarchal institution that treated women like chattel, and saw sex as a status category with political implications. Differing from Firestone, Millett argued biology/physical state is not really a determining factor for sexual politics; that the sex role has little to do with biology, but mostly to do with social conditioning. Millett submitted that the patriarchal myth is that the sex role imposed upon women is natural and maternal, but in reality little but the plumbing is natural. She wrote that the traditional roles, behaviors, attitudes, and oppression were now being challenged by education and industrialization. She used the writing of D.H. Lawrence, Henry Miller, and Norman Mailer as examples of male literature propagating the sexual roles.

She also attributed family patriarchy as the model for social patriarchy. She wrote that sexual identity thought was generally impressed upon an individual by 18 months, and sexual behavior had largely to do with learning, not instinct. She asserted the notion that chivalry—which was no substitute for the social standing and opportunity denied to women—served as a distraction from one's actual status. Millett also charged that rape was a weapon for patriarchy, a tool for dominance and oppression by which women have learned to accept the subordinate position. She equated patriarchy with property, matriarchy with socialism.

Sexual Politics became an overnight commercial and critical success. Kate Millett was thrust into limelight in the press, who wanted to create a spokesperson within the women's liberation movement. Others among the radical feminists opposed the elevation of Millett's status, as rifts began to develop around those women who attained some level of success and celebrity through their work in the women's movement. Things escalated in December of that year when *Time* magazine revealed that Millett was bisexual. Several members of NOW spoke out in support of Millett, but homosexuality remained a divisive issue within the women's movement.

Women and the Media

By 1970, the women's movement had begun branching out into new forms of media, including TV, music, and print journalism. Women also began to take issue with the mainstream press. On January 27, 1970, in a media event which would come to be known as the "shot heard round the left," radical feminists took over the editorial offices of the perennial underground newspaper, *RAT Subterranean News*, which regularly featured sexist ads, language, and graphics. Robin Morgan seemed to write the epitaph for the male New Left movement when she penned "Goodbye to All That," which appeared in *Rat* on February 7, 1970. Calling for a break from the chauvinistic Left, Morgan wrote:

> It seems obvious that a legitimate revolution must be led by, made by those who have been most oppressed: black, brown, and white women . . .
>
> The oppressors are indeed fucked up by being masters (racism hurts whites, sexual stereotypes are harmful to men) but those masters are not oppressed . . . sexism is not the fault of women . . .
>
> There is something every woman wears around her neck on a thin chain of fear—an amulet of madness. For each of us there exists somewhere a moment of insult so intense that she will reach up and rip the amulet off, even if the chain tears at the flesh of her neck (Alpert 1990, 244).

Also by this time, the emergence of the feminist press had grown more and more pronounced, with more than two dozen other feminist periodicals in publication. Besides the *Voice of Women's Liberation* in Chicago, *No More Fun and Games* in Boston, *and Notes from the Second Year* in New York, these also included *Off Our Backs*, from Washington DC, *Lilith* from Seattle's Women's Majority Union; the *Women's Action Movement* in Madison, Wisconsin, *Tooth and Nail* from the Bay Area Women's Liberation, the *Women's Liberation Newsletter* in Cambridge, Massachusetts; *Spazm* and *It Ain't Me, Babe,* from Berkeley, California; *Women, a Journal of Liberation* in Baltimore, Maryland, and *Ain't I a Woman* from Iowa. It seemed clear that no one could remain oblivious to the women's movement for long.

Martha Allen in *History of Women's Media*, identified eight characteristics of early pioneering feminist media:

1. women speaking for themselves, not reporting others
2. preference for collective rather than hierarchical structures
3. sharing instead of competing
4. analysis of mass media's role relative to women and women's media
5. nonattack approach, no name-calling or discrimination
6. open forum emphasis
7. provision of information not reported by mass media
8. activist orientation

At the same time, increasing coverage of women's liberation by the mainstream media created—often unwittingly—unofficial spokespersons and media stars out of women such as Kate Millett, Robin Morgan, Ti-Grace Anderson, and Shulamith Firestone. The women were often writers themselves, whose personal careers clearly benefited from the public notoriety. Those who gained that notoriety were often deemed as "elitist," creating rifts between them and other members of the women's movement.

Essays about Women's Roles

In 1971, a new wave of new feminist literature flooded the market, mostly through the New York Radical Women's newsletter, *Notes from the Third Year*. Among the essays released that year included:

"Getting Angry" by Susi Kaplow

Kaplow advocated consciousness-raising around anger, from individual to group to society. Kaplow insisted that many women were furious at men, but in this society women were not allowed to get angry. She writes that anger meant self-confidence, and removed women from the role of constant mediator.

"Women in the Middle" by Florence Rush

This essay prophesied the Sandwich Generation, a term used to refer to people caring for aging parents while still supporting their own children. It described the responsibility women shoulder for dependents, and argued that women must learn to say no to that role.

"Loving Another Woman" by Ann Koedt

Koedt contrasted the difference between men and women in sexual relationships. She wrote that men equate sex with conquest, rather than an expression of affection and love. She advocated against gender roles in favor of equal partners who emphasize feelings and sensuality. She lamented the difficulty of expressing affection in public, and discussed how feminism and gay liberation deal with sex role conformity.

A Feminist Look at Children's Books

This essay from an anthology on *Radical Feminism* examined sex roles in children's books, and discussed how "Sex prejudice is the only prejudice now considered socially acceptable." It describes how a weeping boy is called a sissy, and how girls are expected to give up "tomboy" ways at adolescence. It asserts how men are rarely depicted as talking with feeling, doing household chores, or raising children. It focused on the sexist roles both boys and girls are compelled to fill. This quote from *Miracles on Maple Hill* by Virginia Sorenson, (Harcourt, 1956), cited in "A Feminist Look at Children's Books," is an example:

> For the millionth time she was glad she wasn't a boy. It was all right for girls to be scared or silly or even ask dumb questions.

Everyone just laughed and thought it was funny. But if anyone caught Joe asking a dumb question and even thought he was the littlest bit scared, he went red and purple and white. Daddy was even something like that, old as he was (Sorenson Koedt, 98). (Sorenson 1956)

"The Building of the Gilded Cage" by Jo Freeman

Freeman discussed the social control and perpetual tutelage which, she argued, keep women as children in the patriarchal society. She examined the *Patria potestus*, or "power of the father," which is transferred to the husband in marriage, causing women to lose not only their own names, but control over their own bodies. She discussed how labor protection laws had been used to limit the hours of women in corporations, and thus limit their upward mobility. She further wrote about how most women thoroughly internalized the social division, and refused to recognize the oppression: "No other minority so thoroughly accepts the standards of the dominant group as its own and interprets any deviance from those values as a sign of degeneracy" (Freeman 1973, 139). She discusses how this gilded cage pervades cross-culturally, and is exerted during adolescence, which is when women tend to fall behind in obtaining opportunities within society.

MS. Magazine and the Mainstream Press

Finally, on December 6, 1971, *The New York* magazine ran a sample insert of a magazine called *MS.*, a landmark institution in both women's liberation and American journalism. Under founding editor Letty Cottin Pegrebin, *MS.* debuted with articles on "housewife's moment of truth"; desexing the English language; and abortion, while most women's magazines at the time featured articles on subjects such as marriage, children, and cosmetics. When the first regular issue hit newsstands in July 1972, television broadcaster Harry Reasoner reportedly predicted it would survive six months. *MS.* magazine sold 300,000 issues in eight days; generating 26,000 subscription orders, and receiving more than 20,000 reader letters within weeks. It would be called the "first national magazine to make feminist voices audible, feminist journalism tenable, and a feminist world view available to the public" (*MS. Magazine*, 2007).

Although *MS.* would have a cofounder in Robin Morgan, and an editor in Ellen Willis, its most famous personality would be a 37-year-old reporter and NOW member named Gloria Steinham. Known for the article called *A Bunny's Tale*, depicting the treatment of women at the Playboy Club, she had published a groundbreaking article in *Esquire* magazine in 1962 on women who have to choose between marriage and career. Although she would by decade's end become the face of feminism in America, many radical feminists felt Steinham and the magazine had no radical credibility. Steinham would be seen as steering the movement toward a watered down, conservative feminism, avoiding the male-domination-oppression theme, which linked oppression of women to the economic system at large. Indeed, to be a viable commercial commodity, it seemed *MS.* was willing to play ball within the paternalistic, capitalistic system which the radical feminists so heartily opposed. Even the advertisements in *MS.* were considered commercialism colored in feminism. As such, *MS.* would be able to bring feminist ideas and issues to a larger audience than ever before but, as some saw it, at the price of co-opting the radical feminist edge. The success of *MS.* would be indicative of the mainstreaming of the feminist movement, a shift from the radical feminism of the 1960s to the pull-yourself-up-by-your-bootstraps liberal feminism of the 1970s.

Unlike other radical feminists, Kathie Sarachild initially defended the magazine, acknowledging the need for the women's movement to draw support from "respectable" women. But by 1975, Sarachild and other members of the radical group the Redstockings would label Steinham and *MS.* a CIA front to stop the radical feminist movement. Ellen Willis would resign from *MS.* the same year, claiming *MS.* to be a political organization, which was unduly seen as the center of the women's movement. Many radical feminists resented Steinham's coronation as spokesperson for movement. And some radical feminist writers envied the success of *MS.*, which used writers outside the radical feminist universe.

MS., along with the articles Betty Friedan started writing for *McCalls*, further moved the movement toward the mainstream. They warned of misguided zeal of the radical feminists and their divisive power struggle, which encouraged the polarization of men and women and created rifts among women of diverse backgrounds. They said the label of "feminist" could be as debilitating as "supermom." Side by side

McCall's and *MS.* played a crucial role in making the women's movement palatable to women in middle America.

Feminism and Religion: Mary Daly's *Beyond God the Father*

In 1973, Boston College theology professor Mary Daly released the second of her groundbreaking and controversial works, *Beyond God the Father*, which followed her first book, *The Church and the Second Sex* (1968). Initially a reformist, Mary Daly felt the oppression of women began in the most basic institution, religion, and proposed not only a spiritual space for women, but a feminist-based theology.

Daly condemned the Roman Catholic Church specifically—and most of the world's religious system in general—as an institution of oppression and deceptions, sanctifying the passivity of women with the promise of happiness in heaven:

> I came to see that all of the so-called major religions from Buddhism and Hinduism to Islam, Judaism, and Christianity, as well as such secular derivatives as Freudianism, Jungianism, Marxism, and Maoism—are mere sects, infrastructures of the edifice of patriarchy (Bridle 2009, 1).

She wrote that the church supported the notion of the natural inferiority of women, who are compelled to identify with Mary the Virgin Mother of God, rather than any image of Divinity itself. She also criticized the exclusion of women from church hierarchy, perpetuating the inferiority complex. Daly offered two basic questions to challenge the patriarchal religious system: (1) Is God really male? and (2) Does God really ordain the subordination of women? She developed the theological perspective "Post-Christian Radical Feminism," while garnering a reputation as one of the most daring and unconventional of all feminists. She became recognized as the grande dame of feminist theologian scholarship.

Works Cited

"A Feminist Look at Children's Books," in *Radical Feminism*, Anne Koedt, ed., New York: Quadrangle Books, 1973.

Alpert, Jane, *Growing Up Underground*, New York: Citadel Press, 1990, 244.

Bair, Deirdre, *Simone de Beauvoir: A Biography*, New York: Summit Books, 1990, 388.

Berkeley, Kathleen C., *The Women's Liberation Movement in America*, Westport, CT: Greenwood Press, 1999, 41.

Bridle, Susan, "No Man's Land: An Interview with Mary Daly" June–August 2009, http://www.enlightennext.org/magazine/j16/daly.asp.

Beauvoir, Simone, *The Second Sex*, New York: Alfred A Knopf, 1952, xxx–679.

Brown, Jenny, "Gainesville-area Women's Liberation pioneers honored in NYC," February 1998, http://www.afn.org/iguana/archives/1998_02/19980206.html.De.

Echols, Alice, *Daring to Be Bad, Radical Feminism in America, 1967–1975*, Minneapolis: University of Minnesota Press, 1989, 31.

Firestone, Shulameth, *The Dialectic of Sex*, New York: William Morrow and Company, Inc., 1970, 12.

Freeman, Jo, *The Bitch Manifesto*, April 1997, http://scriptorium.lib.duke.edu/wlm/bitch.

Freeman, Jo, *The Building of the Gilded Cage*, 1971, Koedt, Anne, Radical Feminism, New York: Quadrangle Books, 139.

Friedan, Betty, *The Feminist Mystique*, New York: W.W. Norton & Company, 1963, 33.

HerStory: 1971–Present, 2007, http://www.msmagazine.com/about.asp.

Jones, Beverly, and Judith Brown, *Toward a Female Liberation Movement*, Gainesville, FL, 1968, 4, 19, 25.

King, Mary, and Casey Haden, "Sex and Caste: A Kind of Memo," *Liberation*, April 1966, 47.

Moi, Toril, *Simone de Beauvoir: The Making of an Intellectual Woman*, Oxford: Blackwell, 1994, 24.

Weisstein, Naomi, "Kinder, Kuche, Kirche as Scientific Law: Psychology Constructs the Female," Boston: New England Free Press, 1968, 10.

Weisstein, Naomi, "Power, Resistance, and Science," *New Politics*, Winter 1997, 2.

CHAPTER TWO

Groups,
Organizations,
and Beliefs

The radical feminists were not one united front of women. Rather, they were comprised of a wide variety of groups with a spectrum of philosophies and agenda.

The National Organization for Women (NOW)

Betty Friedan, author of *The Feminine Mystique*, stepped further into the forefront of liberation for women when she was named the founding president of the National Organization for Women (NOW), in Washington, DC in October of 1966. Three hundred women and men signed on as members, creating what was then touted as the NAACP for women. Besides Friedan, other founding officers for NOW included Kay Clarenbach (who became NOW's first chairperson), and Pauli Murray, the first African American female priest of the Episcopal Church, at the age of 62.

Murray reportedly had contacted Friedan when both women attended a conference in Washington in June 1966 called "Targets for Action." One of the targets had become the Equal Employment Opportunity Commission (EEOC), which was formed in 1965 to enforce the Civil Rights Act of 1964. However, in September 1965, the EEOC had voted to allow sex discrimination in job advertising, by a vote of 3–2. Murray met with Friedan to begin discussions about how to convince the EEOC of the error of its ways. Murray, Friedan, and others then met to discuss creating a civil rights organization for women, to combat exactly the kinds of injustices the EEOC was practicing. NOW would create seven task forces which define it national agenda: Equal Opportunity of Employment; Legal and Political Rights; Education; Women in Poverty; The Family; Image of Women; Women and Religion. But despite Friedan's tentative start as president, NOW would eventually grapple with more controversial causes, such as lesbianism, abortion, and the ERA.

NOW would also construct a Bill of Rights, naming six campaigns for the organization to support: enforcement of laws banning sex discrimination; maternity leave rights in employment and in social security benefits; tax deduction for home and child care expenses for working parents; child-care centers; equal and integrated education; and equal opportunities for job training, housing, and family allowances for women in poverty.

At the outset, the New York chapter of NOW had a more radical persona than the more middle-of-the-road mother organization. In 1967, a fiery feminist from Louisiana named Ti-Grace Atkinson joined NOW, at age 28, with no prior political experience. She became president of the New York chapter of NOW, which at the time boasted 30 percent of NOW membership and included Rita Mae Brown. But within a year, both Brown and Atkinson would leave NOW, after Friedan took a conservative stand on lesbianism. Friedan was afraid of NOW being viewed as a fringe group, out of touch with the larger community of women. Atkinson criticized the hierarchical, nondemocratic structure of NOW, questioning how one can change a societal structure from an organization that politically supports that structure. She also challenged NOW's unwillingness to combat churches—particularly Catholic churches—over the issue of abortion.

NOW would eventually become a more inclusive organization, inviting a wide spectrum of participants, including the gay community, as the realization dawned that a diverse movement might be more valuable than a united one. NOW allowed each individual woman to relate to the movement in the way most appropriate for her life.

NOW would grow to be more respectable and easier to find than the small groups, and would come to prefer reform of the present system to revolution, and move from political action to consciousness-raising. Between 1967 and 1974, NOW would grow from the one New York chapter to seven hundred nationwide, and from one thousand members to more than 40 thousand.

NOW's major struggles historically have been with structure, not ideology. Because it began as a national organization, it often had trouble organizing local, grassroots groups. But for the radical feminists—those whose aim would be to tear down and rebuild society to eliminate the oppression of women—NOW would prove insufficient to meet their revolutionary goals.

The National Conference on New Politics and the Chicago Women's Liberation Union (CWLU)

On Labor Day Weekend of 1967, the Students for a Democratic Society organized the National Conference on New Politics at Palmer House in Chicago. More than two thousand delegates gathered with the purpose of fostering unity within the New Left movement, which had begun to be divided by factionalism between men and women, and between blacks and whites. More than four dozen women attended the conference together, in which a general resolution of civil rights for women emerged.

A series of women's caucuses had been scheduled and cancelled but finally the workshop materialized on the final day of the conference. With the leadership of Jo Freeman and Shulamith Firestone, the women from the caucus issued a resolution, advocating the end of women as sex objects; the revamping of marriage, divorce, and property laws to assure greater equality for women; support for the dissemination of birth control information, and the removal of prohibitions on abortion. Although the resolution was scheduled for presentation before the delegates, at the last moment it was pulled from the agenda. When Firestone stepped forward to protest, conference chair William Pepper reportedly patted Firestone on the head condescendingly, saying, "Move on, little girl; we have more important issues to talk about here than women's liberation" (Berkeley 1999, 44).

This conference created the impetus for the first autonomous women's liberation group in the country, the Chicago Women's Liberation Union (CWLU). The CWLU met for the first time the following week

Chicago Women's Liberation Union members, Chicago, Illinois, 1974. (Chicago History Museum, Photographer Elaine Wessel, ICHi-37477)

in Chicago, and Vivian Rothstein became its first staff person. Chicago was, according to Ti-Grace Atkinson, "for a long time, the heart of the women's movement" (Atkinson 1974, 98). The CWLU was "organized as a union of locals, each engaged in its own activities such as producing the organization's newsletter, running the abortion service, a graphics collection, a liberation school" (Kesselman 1998, 46).

In March of 1966, the CWLU would publish *The Voice of Women's Liberation*, the first newsletter by a major women's liberation organization. *The Voice of Women's Liberation* was written in the first person, featuring a different editor for each issue. It became a major medium for the communication of radical feminist thought for the next 16 months, until publication stopped in June 1969.

JANE: The Abortion Network

Out of the Chicago area grew the legendary underground abortion referral network called JANE. Begun by Heather Tobis Booth and supported by the Westside Group, the CWLU, and other women's groups, it started informally in 1965. JANE facilitated more than

10 thousand abortions—some self-administered—in Chicago during the seven years before *Roe v. Wade*.

Key Questions of the Movement

By this time, the need for a separate women's movement was being recognized by women of the New Left. Among the questions that the women would address was whether the adversary was actually men, or the capitalistic system which supported male supremacy. Ann Koedt, for example, believed the problem went beyond "the system," because women are always secondary to men. She and others believed that all women were oppressed by men, and that the nuclear family—supported by the Judeo-Christian ethic—was the cornerstone of male supremacy. Women were the proletariat of the family. The women would begin to struggle with whether the focus of the women's movement should be consciousness-raising among women, or political action to change the system. The women also began to look at how heterosexual sex—the need for intercourse—reassured male supremacy, and how lesbianism paved a way to intensify the struggle against male supremacy. In any case, the exclusion of men from an autonomous women's movement was becoming an increasingly acceptable idea.

The Movement Gains Ground

The New York Radical Women (NYRW), founded in October of 1967 by Firestone and Pam Allen, became a jumping-off point for many radical feminists, groups, and causes. These included The Feminists, New York Radical Feminists, and the street theater group WITCH. Included among the members of NYRW were Corinne Coleman, who was the editor of a short-lived women's liberation magazine called *Feelings*, and Peggy Dobbins, a member of the Southern Student Organizing Committee. There were also Sheila Cronan (author of *Marriage*, 1970) and Jennifer Gardner, who helped found the San Francisco Bay Area's Women's Liberation publication, *The Women's Page*. Irene Peslikis—a major proponent of consciousness-raising and the feminist line—wrote the article, "Resistances to Consciousness-raising," and became editor of the journal, *Women & Art*. Patricia Mainardi wrote

The Politics of Housework. Barbara Mehroff became part of the circle of support for fugitive-to-be Jane Alpert. These women felt ostracized, trivialized, and abandoned on the periphery of the New Left Movement. They saw similarities between Black Power and Women Power, and felt that women needed their own civil rights movement.

The New York Radical Feminists

The New York Radical Feminists (NYRF) were founded by Shulamith Firestone and Ann Koedt in the fall of 1969 as a "mass based radical feminist movement." The hand-picked initial members—including Minda Bikman, Diane Crothers, Marsha Gershin, Cellestine Ware—divided up into brigades taking names of early suffragists, with the Firestone-Koedt brigade becoming the Stanton-Anthony brigade. Firestone tried to instill a three-month training system of consciousness-raising and reading of radical feminist history. Women had to apply for full-time membership, and Firestone and Koedt were attacked as elitist and dictatorial. Eventually the pair left the NYRF, and in fact Firestone rather abruptly left the entire women's movement. Remaining members seemed more interested in self-actualization than restructuring of society. The NYRF would continue to sponsor events through 1974, although the focus of the group moved to individual brigades.

The Radical Feminists Split from NOW

A wide gap existed between the feminists—those who wanted to raise consciousness about the societal plight of women, and the politicos—who wanted to focus energies on changing what appeared to be a sexist, injustice culture for women. The gap widened further in October 17, 1968. Baton Rouge-born Ti-Grace Atkinson, president of the New York Chapter of NOW, left NOW to launch what would become known as the October 17, or The Feminists, in 1969. She would soon be joined by other disaffected feminists, including Lila Karp, Nanette Rainone, Anne Kalderman, Sheila Cronan, Marcia Winslow, Linda Feldman, and Pam Kearon, at whose Greenwich Village apartment the group would sometimes meet.

At this point, Betty Friedan—president of the national NOW—had begun to steer NOW toward the middle of the road. She became increasingly concerned with the image of the women's movement, unwilling to risk alienating what she saw as important communities of women. Radical feminists such as Atkinson objected to the top-down, hierarchical structure of NOW, which mimicked the oppressive male system which they struggled to change. Atkinson also particularly took issue with the unwillingness of NOW to confront churches—particularly the Catholic church—over the issue of abortion. Atkinson would condemn the failure of consistency within the women's movement, something she tried to instill within The Feminists. She would insist on a quota of no more than one-third of members who were married, and asserted that, indeed, women are a political class.

The Feminists came to identify the female problem of acquiescence to the male-dominated system. To The Feminists, the personal was indeed political, and The Feminists steered their members toward cultural feminism, that is, the business of creating a separate culture for feminism. The Feminists urged women to change, with no quiescence to social style. They set strong standards for female behavior, rejected biological reasons for accepting stereotypical roles, often making married women feel like the enemy. They asserted that sex roles must be destroyed—not the people who occupy them—and that heterosexual sex merely reassures male supremacy. They preached that vaginal intercourse was unneeded for women, that the need for sex was a delusion which distracted women from obtaining completeness within themselves, which eliminated the illusion of the need for men. At the same time, they believed the one thing men feared was sexual irrelevance.

The Feminists personified the radical feminist wing of the women's movement, as all of its members came from the lower or lower-middle class except for Atkinson. Atkinson became identified by media as the leader, but in April of 1970 the group essentially censured Atkinson, deciding no member could speak with the media without prior approval. Steps were taken to keep Atkinson from monopolizing the meetings, which spoiled the egalitarian ideal. Atkinson would eventually leave, but the group would continue to pass rules about tardiness, attendance, and behavior, including drugs and alcohol. Still pushing separatism, The Feminists preached that sex was more of a distraction than anything else, important only as related to topics such as rape, marriage, or prostitution. By 1970, the group began studying female religion and matriarchy. Sheila Cronan left in 1971 for law school, while The Feminists finally disbanded by late 1973.

Cell 16 Advocates Cultural Feminism

At the same time that The Feminists were developing in New York, the city of Boston found itself the home of the Boston Women's Liberation, which would come to be known as Cell 16. The etymology of the name seems to have one of two sources: the first is that it was named after the address member Abbie Rockefeller, at 16 Lexington Avenue in Boston, which became a gathering place for Cell 16. The second story claims the member of Cell 16 saw themselves as one cell in a growing movement. In any case, Cell 16 became the first prominent women's liberation organization to advocate separate, cultural feminism.

The founder of Cell 16 was a 30-year-old woman from rural Oklahoma named Roxanne Dunbar. Dunbar gathered Dana Densmore, Abby Rockefeller, Jeanne Lafferty; Lisa Leghorn, Jayne West, and Betsy Warrior into Cell 16. They formed what has been called the quintessential radical women's liberation group, adhering to the concepts of celibacy, separatism, and Marxism. Dunbar reportedly told the group, "We shall not fight on the enemy's grounds" (Echols 1989, 159).

Cell 16 held that all women were oppressed by men; that family was the cornerstone of male supremacy, and women were the proletariat of the family. They maintained a policy of speaking only to women reporters. Dunbar predicted women's liberation would overcome the entirety of the movement, which ultimately would want to destroy the three pillars of class: family, private property, and the state.

Cell 16 members believed that conventional women's behavior was due to sexual conditioning. They believed that interest in sex, fashion, makeup, and children indicated a collaboration with the oppressive system. Cell 16 members regularly wore khaki pants, work shirts, combat boots, and short hair. Densmore asserted that women must stop believing in their own inferiority, and their conditioned dependence on men. After Abby Rockefeller used her Tae Kwon Do to subdue a male attacker one late November 1968 night, Cell 16 members began studying self-defense techniques.

Cell 16 members considered a celibate to be a lucid person, stating that sex is a minor need blown out of proportion by men. The Cell never actually advocated lesbianism per se, just celibacy and separation from men, personally and politically. They implied that sex was unnatural, and only a personal, temporary solution to the misery of society. Densmore, in particular, preached that sex was only appropriate for reproduction, and that healthy people don't like being touched. She said physical pleasure was more of an issue for men. Members adhered to the paradox that advocated the elimination of sex, but also said maternalism is the cornerstone of female principle, which all people must develop. They stated that pornography illustrated male power over women, and that male characteristics created the chaotic, violent, greedy world unknown in matriarchal societies.

In October of 1968, Cell 16 released *No More Fun and Games*, with contributions by Dana Densmore, Lisa Leghorn, and Betsy Warrior. This became what many considered the first theoretical journal of the women's movement. It included articles on sexism, self-defense, sexuality, celibacy, and a critique of traditional women's magazines published by men.

Women's International Terrorist Conspiracy from Hell (Witch)

Created by Robin Morgan, Peggy Dobson, Florika Romatien, Naomi Jaffe and others, the concept of WITCH (Women's International Terrorist Conspiracy from Hell) grew out of New York City, and spread throughout the movement. Wild and irreverent, using the venue of guerilla street theater, WITCH create awareness of radical feminist issues through active skits, using drama and humor. WITCH made its initial dramatic entry into the movement on Halloween night of 1968, as members dressed in bright masks, fright makeup, and rags, gathered in front of Chase Manhattan Bank. With pails and broomsticks in hand, they "hexed" Wall Street and the entire financial district. Robin Morgan, who called WITCH more of an idea in action than an organization, more of a method than a group, recalled later that the Dow Jones Industrial Average declined sharply that day. The antics of WITCH spread to other venues on other dates. On Valentine's Day in 1969, they hexed the Bridal Fair in New York, to "Confront the Whoremakers." In Boston the women hexed bars; in Washington, DC they hexed the Presidential Inauguration. In Chicago WITCH zapped multiple targets, including the Sociology

Department of the University of Chicago, at the firing of Marlene Dixon. On Halloween in 1969 the target was the trial of New Left Leaders, the Chicago Seven, arrested on charges of conspiracy to riot at the 1968 Democratic Convention. WITCH hexed on Mother's Day, and they hexed the telephone company. Although WITCH drew greater media attention to the women's movement, it also seemed to alienate some women with its over-the-top antics.

Differences between Black Women and White Women

The 1st National Women's Liberation Conference was held in Sandy Springs, Maryland, in November 1968. Organized by Kathie Sarachild and Carol Hanisch of NYRW, and Judith Brown and Carol Giardini of Gainesville Women's Liberation, the conference gathered 22 women from New York, Boston, Chicago, Washington, DC, Baltimore, and Gainesville. The focus of the group was to determine the primary enemy of women's liberation: capitalism or men. Efforts were made by organizers to include black militant women, to get different cultural views of women's liberation, but those efforts were met with resistance. Organizers wanted to open up the definition of women's oppression, and a successful effort might have challenged the mythical "universal" experience of women, allowing a greater diversity within the movement earlier. But many called the integration effort a dreadful mistake, as it seemed to hasten the dissipation of the radical feminist movement.

A rift between white women and black women had seemed to form within the women's movement from the beginning. The spectrum between mere tolerance and actual acceptance was challenged in both directions. According to Kathleen Berkeley, white women early on often saw black women as role models, finding them just as capable within their organizations as white men. At the same time, black women seemed to keep distant from white women, often seen as competition due to sexual entanglements among blacks and whites during the civil rights movement. From the outset, black women did not seem to respond to the King and Casey manifesto, *Sex and Caste: A Kind of Memo*. It was thought that for African Americans, racial discrimination was the bigger issue, with sexual discrimination a secondary concern. Said Echols, "Middle-class women were struggling for these things—independence and self-sufficiency—which racial and class oppression had thrust upon black women (Echols 1989, 33).

For example, while white women were struggling to find equal opportunities in the work force, women of color had been going to work out of necessity for decades. While white women sought independence from men, black women often had independence thrust upon them, becoming the head of the household without choice. Consciousness-raising of women's liberation was a secondary concern for women struggling to put food on the table.

The rift between the races raised a very basic and significant question: Was women's liberation primarily a white woman's cause? Marlene Dixon seemed to think so:

> Sisterhood temporarily disguised the fact that all women do not have the same interests, needs, desires: working class women and middle class women, student women and professional women, minority women and white women have more conflicting interests than could ever be overcome by their common experience based on sex discrimination. The illusions of sisterhood were possible because Women's Liberation had become in its ideology and politics predominantly a middle class movement.
>
> . . . Women were far too slow to recognize class struggle for what it was within the movement . . . the movement isolated itself . . . from the concrete struggles of working class women, in the home and in the factory, who make up the majority of oppressed and exploited women (Dixon 1977, 11–15).

Toni Morrison, in the *New York Times Magazine* in August 1971, wrote that the "whiteness of the women's liberation movement engendered a deep sense of mistrust in black women. They look at white women and see the enemy—for racism is not confined to white man" (Morrison 1971, SM14).

If there were to be attempts to include women of color, there would have to be recognition that there were class differences in the level of oppression. There would need to be cultural definitions of women's liberation, to determine if liberation was the same for white women and women of color. Many white radical women's groups appeared to assume that since the black movement wanted to separate from the New Left, the black women would want to separate from the white women. Often very few efforts were made to reach across the color barrier.

Barbara Omolade, a black nationalist who became a feminist after working in battered women's shelter in Brooklyn, described her experience of the rift within the feminist movement:

> Feminism has been undermined by white women's unexamined and outrageous acts of racism. White women activists frequently bypassed and ignored the experiences, expertise, and institutions of Black people, while attempting to get black women to work for them . . ."

> Although there were many Black feminists within nationalist organizations, Black women's dominant political consciousness and identity has been always exclusively shaped by Black resistance to racism. However, in the same way that race undermines white women's attempts at creating a viable feminist movement, blindness to the significance of gender blunted the effectiveness of Black politics. By closing off serious examination of gender, Black nationalists have become unable to explore internal divisions and dilemmas that prevent the internal development of an effective political agenda which could benefit all Black people. I am frankly afraid when I hear of some Black nationalist woman's adamant and unexamined put-down of feminism, because I and others have learned about the closeted, silent space of the personal lives of many Black women who have been victimized and humiliated by the sexism of Black men. The avoidance of a gender analysis has allowed Black women to make their actual experiences with Black men. And no matter how they try to comfort, understand, rationalize, or explain Black male violence against Black Women, it can't legitimately be viewed as anything but a stumbling block to Black unity. In fact, much of the divisiveness within the Black community can be directly traced to the unbridled and unexamined expression of Black male chauvinism. And what political framework can we use to explain its raw use of male power and brutality, except feminism? (Omolade 1998, 395–396).

Political Divisions at the Camp Hastings Conference of 1968

A national women's liberation conference assembled at Camp Hastings, Lake Villa, Illinois, on Thanksgiving weekend in November of 1968.

Organizers included Marilyn Webb of DC Women's Liberation, Helen Kritzler of NYRW, and Laya Firestone from Chicago's Westside Group. The initial purpose was to commemorate the 120-year anniversary of the1848 Women's Rights Convention in Seneca Falls, New York.

The conference drew more than two hundred attendees, offering the opportunity for activists in the women's liberation movement to meet others around the country. There Kathie Amatniek (Sarachild) presented her workshop, "A Program for Feminist Consciousness-Raising," in which the concept of consciousness-raising was introduced as an exercise to help women understand how unequal their situations were. Judith Brown of Gainesville Women's Liberation described the experience as follows:

> We usually welcomed interruptions, which often confirmed a collective aspiration of hopes and desires (for real love and good sex, for example) we once thought everyone else had already achieved; or, confirmed as group problems a worry (about pregnancy, for example), emotional pain (about being alone or being left), or economic disaster (about being jobless), we had thought at first was only "my problem." I loved an interruption that gave a different lens to view our hidden experience (Brown 1986, 5).

The conference spotlighted the often bitter factional fighting that had developed between the profeminists of New York and Gainsville, and feminists from the New Left movement (known as politicos) from everywhere else. Of the split Jane Alpert would write, "The politico-feminist split is a real one, one that will vanish as soon as we accept ourselves as women first of all, but which will continue to divide us until we share that consciousness" (Alpert 1990, 4).

The rift between the politicos and the feminists developed largely along the questions of whether women's liberation should remain a part of the New Left movement, or whether women needed a movement of their own. Those from the politico camp asserted that the oppression of women stemmed from the societal oppression of the proletariat from the capitalistic system. They asserted that the pro-women line may have exaggerated men's power and women's powerlessness. The politicos believed the women's movement should be a wing of the Left, and connected to a larger movement. The upending of the capitalistic system required a united commitment, and the ability to organize within the New Left. As Dixon put it:

> The feminist line stemmed from the assertion that "men are the principal enemy" and that the primary contradiction is between men and women. The politico line stemmed from the assertion that the male supremacist ruling class is the principal enemy and the primary contradiction exists between exploited and exploiting classes, in which women bear the double burden of economic exploitation and social oppression. The leftist line stressed that the object of combat against male-supremacist practices was the unification of the men and women of the exploited classes against a common class enemy in order to transcend the division and conflict sexism between them (Dixon 1977, 8).

Different Approaches to Consciousness-Raising

Among the practitioners of consciousness-raising, there were differences in approach. Some, like Kathie Sarachild, tended to be confrontational, asking questions and challenging assumptions. Others such as Pam Allen, who helped found the San Francisco's Sudsofloppen and NYRW and wrote *Free Space,* emphasized a "free space," a nonjudgmental atmosphere where a woman could express herself and explore her notions at her own pace.

Another disparity between the groups involved support for action versus consciousness-raising, as if the two were mutually exclusive. Those who supported consciousness-raising activities felt it was important for a woman to take the time to understand her situation, and the different ways oppression governed her life. The politicos, however, felt an urgency to take "action," efforts and events which furthered the revolution of the oppressive capitalistic system that fostered the further oppression of women. They also felt the pursuit of a personal solution diluted the revolutionary drive; it was the collective struggle versus personal life improvement.

"The Myth of the Vaginal Orgasm"

Another highlight of the conference was a workshop facilitated by Ti-Grace Atkinson and Ann Koedt, entitled "The Myth of Vaginal Orgasm." In it, Atkinson and Koedt asserted that even sexual intercourse was an oppressive act, because it focused on the needs and wants of the male, and not the female. The workshop challenged the myth that intercourse is as good for the female as for the male. They presented intercourse as the very basic kind of discrimination against females, and the foundation of questioning sex, and everything else that stems from it. They advocated liberation at the most basic level, and encouraged women to question what is considered to be "normal." In her essay of the same name, Koedt wrote, "Women have been defined sexually in terms of what pleases men; our own biology has not been properly analyzed . . . What we must do is redefine our sexuality. We must discard the 'normal' concepts of sex and create new guidelines which take into account mutual sexual enjoyment" (Koedt 1968, 11).

Additional Views on Sex, Marriage, and Dating

The workshop encouraged other ideas and advocacy of revolution. Dana Densmore of Boston's Cell 16 used the workshop to advance the cause of celibacy. Shulamith Firestone from NYRW asserted pregnancy is physically debilitating and inevitably oppressive. Corrine Coleman, also of NYRW, offered an "Alternatives to Marriage" workshop, while Naomi Webster and Marlene Dixon discussed how most women were still caught in the struggle to "get a man."

The Redstockings

In January of 1969, a demonstration was organized to protest the inauguration of President Richard Nixon. It worsened political divisions within the movement and deepened hostilities between the movement and the New Left. With the ugliness of the Counter-Inaugural, resolve to separate the women's movement from the Left deepened. From the aftermath came the formation of Redstockings. Formed by Ellen Willis and Shulamith Firestone, the Redstockings was based on a militant, independent, and radical feminist consciousness. The Redstockings was designed to commemorate the values of socialism and the memory of nineteenth century feminists, who were called Blue Stockings. Other members of the Redstockings included Irene Peslikis, Barbara Mehrhof, Sheila Cronan, Barbara Kamisky (also in The Feminists), Pat Mainardi (*Politics of Housework*), Linda Feldman, and Pam Kearon.

Often meeting in an apartment on the Lower East Side, the Redstockings popularized consciousness-raising, invented the Speak Out, and distributed needed literature on a wealth of topics. The topics for exploration included consciousness-raising, monogamy v. free love, the repression of women by all men, male fidelity v. breaking off all relationships with men, and the need for heterosexual sex as fabrication by men to keep women in line. The Redstockings would become known for its campaign against abortion laws. The Redstockings struggled with the issue of political action v. consciousness-raising—the collective struggle v. personal life improvement. They also dealt with what they saw as a power imbalance; they believed men oppressed women for material gain, and female behavior was due to material circumstances.

The downfall of the Redstockings—and of the radical feminists in general—may have been the assumption that all women's experiences were similar. They did not adequately take into account race, or alternative lifestyle, and thus became primarily white and middle class. As it reemerged in 1975, the Redstockings took an anti-alternative lifestyle stand, accusing lesbians and celibates of promoting cultural feminism, taking themselves out of the battle with men. The group was split on the desire for sexual commitment. Today, the Redstockings maintain an archive of feminist resource material.

The Divisive Issue of Homosexuality

The "Lavendar Menace"

As evidenced in the opening ceremonies at the Second Congress to Unite Women, in 1970, the term "Lavender Menace" was used within the movement to refer to lesbian women. It is generally agreed that the term originated with Betty Friedan, but the exact time and locale that she first used it seems to be a matter of debate. Susan Brownmiller claimed to have heard Friedan refer to lesbians as a "lavender herring," and the term morphed from there. However, there seems to be little debate about how Friedan felt about lesbians in the women's movement, as she describes for herself in her memoir *Life So Far:*

> My attitude was I don't want to know; sort of like the current military policy toward homosexuals of "Don't ask, don't tell." I come from Peoria.

The Women's Strike Coalition was planning to hold a press conference, they told me, and declare that we were all lesbians, in solidarity with Kate (Millett) and other bisexuals and lesbians, struggling for liberation in a sexist society. I was vehemently opposed and told them so . . . I was and am against repression of any kind. But I didn't think it was a good tactic in any way. To say, "We are all lesbians," was total bullshit, and I wasn't going to do it (Friedan 2000, 221, 224).

Friedan, the consummate mainstreamer, felt feminism should appeal to the suburban housewife without alienating the heartland. She worked constantly to present feminism in an acceptable manner to middle America. Friedan wanted to work for reforms within the existing system, but feared lesbians would push away mainstream Americans. She felt lesbians—stereotypically thought of as man-haters and antifamily feminists—would become the unflattering image of women's liberation, undermining the credibility of the movement. For three years under Friedan, NOW avoided discussions of lesbianism, which became a major source of divisiveness.

Rosalyn Baxandall explained that many within the women's movement remained insensitive to the lesbian contingent: "So we weren't sensitive enough to the fact that there are different kinds . . . that some women loved women, and we should have been more sensitive" (Ceballos 1991, 44).

One of the most important outcomes of the Second Congress to Unite Women was the distribution of a paper entitled "The Woman-Identified Woman," published by a group called the "Radicalesbians" and reportedly written by Rita Mae Brown and Artemis March. The paper discussed the contempt in which women—or those who play the female role—are held, and how women in the movement have in most cases gone to great lengths to avoid discussion and confrontation with the issue of lesbianism. Yet the time had come to bring the issue to light:

> Lesbian is a label invented by the Man to throw at any woman who dares to be his equal, who dares to challenge his prerogatives (including that of all women as part of the exchange medium among men), who dares to assert the primacy of her own needs . . .

... And yet, in popular thinking, there is really only one essential difference between a lesbian and other women: that of sexual orientation—which is to say, when you strip off all the packaging, you must finally realize that the essence of being a "woman" is to get fucked by men ...

... As long as male acceptability is primary—both to individual women and to the movement as a whole—the term lesbian will be used effectively against women. This is because we have internalized the male culture's definition of ourselves. The reason lesbianism is a struggle is because most women are trying to follow what is acceptable to men (Radicalesbians 1970, 2, 3).

At the 2nd Radical People's Constitutional Convention in Philadelphia in the fall of 1970, future members of the Furies Collective furthered the discussion of the role of lesbianism in the movement by claiming that it was not just a sexual orientation, but a political choice: "The woman-identified woman commits herself to other women for political, emotional, physical, and economic support ... not only as an alternative to oppressive male-/female relationships but primarily because she loves women ..." (Freeman 1975, 137).

The Furies Collective

Founded in Washington, DC in May of 1971, The Furies Collective was the most famous (or infamous) of the lesbian-feminist collectives. Often gathering at 221 11th Street in Washington, DC, its membership included Charlotte Bunch, Joan E. Biren, Rita Mae Brown, Sharon Deevey, Ginny Berson, Helaine Harris, and Coletta Reid.

The Furies tried to "take over" the women's movement under mantel of lesbianism-feminism. Most of Furies had once been heterosexual but felt lesbianism was the greatest response to male dominance. They felt that heterosexuality caused a split in the liberation movement between politicos and lesbian-feminist, and saw straight women as the movement's albatross. The Furies saw lesbianism not just as a sexual orientation but a political choice. Furies saw themselves as the vanguard cadre when most women refused to "come out."

Charlotte Bunch wrote the inaugural essay on the Furies Collective, called "Lesbians in Revolt":

... in revolt because she defines herself in terms of women and rejects the male definitions of how she should feel, act, look and live. The Lesbian threatens the ideology of male supremacy by destroying the lie about female inferiority, weakness, passivity, and by denying women's "innate" need for men (Bunch 1972, 1, 3).

In its zeal, the Furies Collective became hermetic, like the Weathermen of the New Left. The Collective became fascist in the demands of its members, often characterized as absolute, dogmatic, and disruptive. Disagreements arose, and creative instinct was squashed. The collective advocated leaving male children with their fathers; the working class within the collective did not want children around at all, because they did not want to raise more.

Rita Mae Brown tried to advance understanding of the women's differences in the collective, but her imperious style reportedly bothered others. The collective dissolved in April of 1972, while The Furies continued in various forms until summer of 1973. Its isolation from the rest of the Washington, DC community may have led to its downfall.

The emergence of lesbian-feminist alliance edged the women's movement from radical feminism—which sought to change the existing culture, toward cultural feminism—which worked to develop a separate culture for women. It challenged the prevailing idea of a universal female experience. It also disputed the concepts of man-hating, as it became understood that while lesbianism became a viable option to heterosexual relationships, many of the problems which affected male-female relationships could be found in lesbian relationships as well.

Support from NOW

On December 8, 1970, a *Time* magazine article revealed that Kate Millett, author of *Sexual Politics: A Manifesto for Revolution*, was bisexual (as if hopeful revelation would discredit the women's movement). Millett had revealed her bisexuality on a panel at a conference on sexual liberation at Columbia University, when a woman confronted her about her sexual orientation. The *Time* article reinforced the views by those skeptics who routinely dismiss all liberationists as lesbian.

In response, Gloria Steinham, Ti-Grace Atkinson, Susan Brownmiller, Florence Kennedy, and other members of NOW—from which Betty Friedan had resigned—held a press conference to support Millett. They asserted that women's liberation and gay liberation were working toward the same goal: to end categorization or stigmatization of individuals by sex or sexual preference. In mid-1971, NOW would finally pass a resolution supporting the lesbian lifestyle.

This was a rather astounding about-face by NOW, who under the presidency of Betty Friedan had worked to suppress the influence of any member who claimed to be a lesbian. This position seemed to signal the dawn of a new era for the women's movement. It acknowledged a new level of acceptance for the gay lifestyle within feminism, but it also revealed the dissipation of the radical edge of the movement, as it sought to be more inclusive of women for varying backgrounds and lifestyles.

At this point, it had become clear that lesbianism had grown to a major issue within the women's movement, symbolizing political will as well as sexual preference. Lesbianism was not just about sex, but about political choice—the choice to not be dependent on a man for anything.

Lesbian Communes

Meanwhile additional lesbian-feminist collectives began developing in spots around the country, besides the Furies Collective. In Washington, DC, former Furies members Joan E. Biren and Sharon Deevy set up the first all-lesbian house called Amazing Grace in the fall of 1971—but it ended after a week due to class division. Tension developed—both within the small communes and outside in the larger movement—amidst the homophobia of heterosexuals and the dogma of lesbians.

But even within the all-female communes, it was noted that some women found themselves in the "male role." Some began to determine that it was the "Male Style" of relationship management that is the enemy, and that same "maleness" could even be found in a lesbian community.

Despite the growing acknowledgement of the gay lifestyle, lesbianism remained a huge issue of division for within the women's movement. Charlotte Bunch of the Furies Collective wrote:

Lesbianism is a threat to the ideological, political, personal, and economic basis of male supremacy . . . The Lesbian's independence and refusal to support one man undermines the personal power that men exercise over women. Our rejection of heterosexual sex challenges male domination in the most individual and common form. We offer women something better than submission to personal oppression. We offer the beginning of the end of collective and individual male supremacy (Echols 1989, 232).

The End of an Era

Between 1972 and 1977, differences between radical and liberal feminism became less obvious:

As the feminist movement matured . . . tactical distinctions between the two branches of feminism became less pronounced. Although equality feminists continued to believe that change came through reforming the system, they were not above borrowing the direct action, protest practices of radical feminists in order to secure the attention of legislators . . . Meanwhile, radical feminists may not have softened their critique of capitalism and patriarchy, but many realized that ideological posturing and protests brought few long-lasting results (Berkeley 1999, 53).

Many of those who refused to move toward the mainstream found solace in cultural feminism, which sought to create separate cultures and communities for women only. Cultural feminism allowed its adherents to withdraw from the struggle against male supremacy, and sought to create a counterculture opposed to seemingly irrevocable male sexism, a haven from male supremacy. The proponents of cultural feminism were more interested in maintaining the alternative culture than building a mass movement.

The tenets of cultural feminism are that women are indeed a unified category, and that men are immutably sexist, seeking to keep women as powerless victims. Cultural feminism provides support and power women need to thrive. Cultural feminism pursues an ideology of self improvement, not social transformation. Cultural feminist critics such as Ellen Willis, Ti-Grace Atkinson, Carol Hanisch, and

Kathie Sarachild say that cultural feminism promotes separatism rather than integration, trading revolution for a kind of mysticism.

Some, such as Mary Daly and Jane Alpert, sought a spiritual theme within cultural feminism. Daly sought a religious transformation to the creative female principle. In her post-Christian radical feminism, Daly foresaw an era when religion would be grounded in a feminist spirituality completely devoid of the oppression and chauvinism which pervaded the majority of organized religions. In *Mother Right*, Jane Alpert saw maternalism as the solution to the problem of women's differences, and that all women—whether mothers or not— could draw from their maternal selves commonalities that could unite all women. Both invoked a vision of the return of the ancient matriarchy, in which economic and political change and the aversion to nuclear annihilation and ecological disaster will follow change of human consciousness. Maternal qualities inherent in men and women would be encouraged to the forefront, as the greed, terror, and oppression of the patriarchy are abated.

Meanwhile, radical feminism had become so caught up in its inner fragmentation—lesbian versus straight, black versus white, wealthy versus poor, politico versus feminist—it seemed to lose sight of the big picture: oppression by men. Those wanting to preserve the myth of unity within the women's movement—with concern about egalitarianism, preserving the collective, and avoiding hierarchy—actually seemed to inhibit the effectiveness. The early movement lacked the flexibility and practical skills needed to endure. As opportunity for women increased, the perceived need for radical feminism decreased.

Many women started turning toward the liberal feminism of NOW, which benefited from disintegration of radical feminism. NOW appeared more accepting of all women, more interested in the liberal reform of society than the radical revolution over it. Under the leadership of NOW and *MS.*, liberal feminism became the recognized voice of women's liberation. It moved from the mantra of "we are one, we are sisters" to recognizing differences among races, classes, and orientations, and creating room for them all. Personal insight into one's own oppression became more important than collective political action. "Personal is political" was originally meant to emphasize the need for political action but ended up emphasizing the personal. Finally traditional "male" values and sex roles became vilified—but not men themselves, so as to not alienate women who chose to remain in relationships with them.

Works Cited

Alpert, Jane, *Growing up Underground*, New York: Citadel Press, 1990, 4.

Atkinson, Ti-Grace, *Amazon Odyssey*, New York: Link Books, 1974, 98.

Berkeley, Kathleen C., *The Women's Liberation Movement in America*, Westport, CT: Greenwood Press, 1999, 44, 53.

Brown, Judith, *Origins of Consciousness-raising in the South: Gainesville or Tampa?*, September 1, 1986, 5.

Bunch, Charlotte, "Lesbians in Revolt," *The Furies*, January 1972, http://scriptorium.lib.duke.edu/wlm/furies/.

Ceballos, Jacqueline Michot, *Interview with Rosalyn Fraad Baxandall*, Cambridge, MA: The Radcliffe Institute for Advanced Study, 1991, 44.

Dixon, Marlene, *The Rise and Demise of Women's Liberation, A Class Analysis*, 1977, www.marxist.org/subject/women/authors/dixon-marlene/rise-demise.htm, 8, 11–15.

Echols, Alice, *Daring to Be Bad: Radical Feminism in America, 1967–1975*, Minneapolis: University of Minnesota Press, 1989, 33, 159, 232.

Freeman, Jo, *The Politics of Women's Liberation*, New York: David McKay Co, 1975, 137.

Friedan, Betty, *Life So Far: A Memoir*, New York: Simon & Schuster, 2000, 221, 248.

Kesselman, Amy, "Our Gang of Four", *The Feminist Memoir Project: Voices from Women's Liberation*, New York: Three Rivers Press, 1998, 46.

Morrison, Toni, "What the Black Woman Thinks about Women's Lib", *New York Times Magazine*, August 1971, SM14.

Omolade, Barbara, "Sisterhood in Black and White", *The Feminist Memoir Project: Voices from Women's Liberation*, New York: Three Rivers Press, 1998, 395–6.

Koedt, Anne, "The Myth of Vaginal Orgasm", New York: *Notes from the First Year*, June 1968, 11.

Radicalesbians, *The Women-Identified Woman*, 1970, http://scriptorium.lib.duke.edu/wlm/womid.

CHAPTER THREE

Protests,
Demonstrations,
and Events

If there was one thing the radical feminists seemed to know how to do, it was protest in a way that brought attention to the cause. Many of the radical feminists were writers and editors with connections to the media, and skillful in organizing media events. Those skills enhanced the delivery of the message, and provided lessons in demonstrations that resonate to this day.

The Jeannette Rankin Brigade

On January 15, 1968, 5 to 10 thousand women joined in what was to be known as the Jeannette Rankin Brigade, in honor of the first woman congressperson of the United States, and the only member of Congress to vote against the United States' entry into World War II. It was called the largest gathering of women for a political purpose since the campaign for the 19th Amendment. Its purpose was to confront Congress on its opening day with a strong show of female opposition to Vietnam War, presenting a petition for immediate withdrawal of troops. Participants included folk singer Judy Collins, Coretta Scott King, and Jeannette Rankin herself, at age 87.

The Jeannette Rankin Brigade, January 15, 1968, Washington, DC. (Bettmann/CORBIS).

However, many came away feeling the demonstration itself was a futile instance of political impotence. Attracting little attention from the press, the brigade seemed to illustrate the subservient invisibility of the women's issue at the time. There was frustration that the women came draped in the role of traditional women, dutifully following the line of dead soldiers as tearful mothers and wives. Shulamith Firestone, in *Notes from the First Year*, described the brigade as "tearful and passive reactors to the actions of men rather than organizing as women to change that definition of femininity to something other than a synonym for weakness, political impotence, and fear" (Firestone 1968, 18). The brigade was criticized for relegating women to a reactionary role to the actions of men, rather than taking action themselves.

In response to the brigade, the NYRW held a funeral and procession for "Traditional Womanhood" at Arlington Seminary. The procession featured a larger-than-life dummy on a transported bier, with disposable items such as S&H Green Stamps, curlers, garters, and hairspray. The demonstration called attention to the passing of the customary notion of appropriate behavior for women.

The Madison Square Garden Bridal Fair Protest

A contingency of 150 women—behind the leadership of WITCH (Women's International Conspiracy from Hell)—infiltrated the Bridal Fair at Madison Square Garden (then known as the Felt Forum) on February 16, 1968, two days after Valentine's Day. Judith Duffett, who worked for *Bride Magazine*, was able to procure tickets for the demonstrators. The protesting women showed up with chains on their legs, dangling products for women from their bridal outfits. Protesters shouted obscenities during the opening address of the Reverend Edmund Mulder. At one point they released reportedly one hundred white mice into the crowd, to add to the pandemonium of the occasion. However, the *New York Times* reported that instead of screaming and panicking, many of the women tried to gather up the mice, to make certain they were not hurt.

The goal of the demonstration was to "confront the whore-makers," a term the protesters used to refer to the capitalists they believed forced and coerced women into stereotypical, Madison-avenue images. Leaflets distributed by WITCH protested "marriage is a dehumanizing institution—legal whoredom for women . . . she is allowed an identity only as an appendage of a man . . ."(Freeman, 2009). But the event seemed to alienate many women in attendance, who objected to being lumped in with prostitutes.

The Seattle Radical Women Protest a Playboy Bunny

By May of 1968, the influence of radical feminism had sprung up throughout the nation. At the University of Washington, Playboy Bunny Reagan Wilson had been scheduled to appear at the campus' annual "Men's Day." The event became a planned protest by the group Seattle Radical Women (SRW).

Before an audience of 450 and wearing paper bags over their heads, members of SRW stormed the stage, chanting satirical lines from the Common Book of Prayer. In defensive response to their activity, a group of men started grabbing, punching, and dragging the women off stage. At that point Barbara Winslow of SRW stepped on stage, in an effort to explain the SRW's point of view. In her first of many public speeches,

Winslow began a "debate" with Reagan Wilson about the ramifications of *Playboy*'s portrayal of women. The debate created an even greater uproar, resulting in the expulsion of Winslow from the stage.

The headline in the University of Washington's Daily newspaper read "Playmate Meets Women—Radical Ones." The banner on Seattle's leading newspaper, *The Post-Intelligencer*, screamed "Guys Gulp, Coeds Sulk at 42-24-36." Winslow would almost immediately be recognized the early spokesperson for the radical woman's movement in Seattle.

Valerie Solanas Shoots Andy Warhol

In June of 1968, a 32-year-old resident of a broken, abusive New Jersey home named Valerie Solanas was catapulted to the symbolic violent fringe of the radical feminist movement. In 1967 Solanas had written the *SCUM Manifesto*, which spoke for the fictitious radical feminist organization called the *Society for Cutting Up Men*, or *SCUM*. The *SCUM Manifesto* (Addendum 3) unleashed a tirade toward the male gender—including the fervent advocacy for the general annihilation of men—with which many women seemed to identify.

But in the afternoon of June 3, 1968, the Solanas rage, so evident in *The SCUM Manifesto,* boiled to overflowing. Solanas burst into the New York studio of iconic artist Andy Warhol, accusing him of appropriating a play she had written *(Up Your Ass)* without sufficient compensation. Solanas shot at Warhol three times with a .32 automatic pistol. The third bullet hit Warhol in the side, penetrating both lungs, his spleen, stomach, and liver. She also shot art critic Mario Amaya. She fled the studio, but then turned herself in to a traffic cop at Times Square.

Solanas was taken to the 13th precinct, brought to Manhattan Criminal Court, and then confined a Bellevue Hospital. On June 28, represented by NOW attorney Flo Kennedy, Solanas was indicted on charges of attempted murder, assault, and illegal possession of a gun. In August she was declared incompetent to stand trial. Later that month, Olympia Press published *The SCUM Manifesto.*

Finally, in June of 1969, Solanas was sentenced to three years in prison. She was released from the New York State Prison for Women in 1971. However, even after her release, she reportedly continued to harass Warhol by telephone and letter.

Valerie Solanas under arrest, June 4, 1968, New York City (Bettmann/CORBIS).

While in prison, Solanas was hailed by many as a super powerful advocate for woman, while others counted her among the criminally insane. Ti-Grace Atkinson, Flo Kennedy, and Roxanne Dunbar visited Solanas at the New York Women's House of Detention. Dunbar characterized the Solanas act "as a signal that a women's liberation movement had begun in the United States" (Dunbar, 1998, 93). Through the Plexiglass window, however, Solanas appeared confused, unstable, and not very communicative through her piercing black eyes.

After her release in 1971, Solanas lived for 17 more years, but died alone in a Tenderloin hotel in San Francisco. It was a far cry from her status in 1968, when she became the radical feminists' first outlaw celebrity.

The 1968 Miss America Protest

Later that year came the event that would come to epitomize the radical feminist activities at their heyday, and would draw fervent national attention to women's liberation. Carol Hanisch of NYRW reportedly came up with idea in the summer of 1968 while watching the feminist film *Schmearguntz*. She explained:

> The idea crept into my head that protesting the pageant in Atlantic City just might be the way to bring the fledgling Women's Liberation Movement into the public arena.
>
> As Ros Baxandall had remarked on the David Susskind TV show, "every day in a woman's life is a walking Miss America contest." It seemed just the boat to start rocking (Hanisch, 1998, 197–198).

On September 7, 1968, more than 150 women traveled from New York, Boston, Washington, DC, Florida, and New Jersey to Atlantic City, to protest what was considered the pinnacle of chauvinist society's demands on women: the annual Miss America Pageant. In front of the Atlantic City Convention Center, the women hurled tokens of their own oppression into the "Freedom Trash Can": high-heeled shoes, curlers, detergent, fake eyelashes, wigs—considered instruments of female torment—as well as copies of *Good Housekeeping* and *Playboy*. They also hung the Master of Ceremonies, Bert Parks, in effigy. The women crowned a live sheep for Miss America. Robin Morgan described the demonstration as an effort to bring awareness to the "appearance issue":

> ... the unbeatable madonna-whore combination: to win approval, we must be both sexy and wholesome, delicate but able to cope, demure yet titillatingly bitchy or should we say ill-tempered ... (American Experience, 1999–2001).

Morgan had organized media coverage, which came out in full force. One of the NYRW members worked for a bridal magazine, and was able to score a block of tickets in the balcony of the convention center. The demonstrators smuggled in a banner, which they unfurled to read "Women's Liberation" while the winner was crowned. The protesters started shouting "No more Miss America!", until finally they were escorted out of the auditorium and into their buses. But interestingly, no one was arrested.

The Miss America Protest, September 7, 1968, Atlantic City, New Jersey (Bettmann/CORBIS).

It was from this event that the indelible image of "bra-burners" became etched in the national collective memory, and became associated with the radical feminists. Someone had apparently told the media that there was an intention to burn bras, which seemed to fuel the idea. In May of that year, NOW members had burned an apron at a Mother's Day demonstration. But in actuality, while several brassieres made it into the Freedom Trash Can, not one bra was actually incinerated at the Miss America Pageant protest.

The Freedom Trash Crash drew nearly six hundred onlookers, many of whom were unsympathetic and increasingly uncomfortable men hostile to the demonstration. These unfriendly observers included male reporters, when it was learned that NYRW would speak only to female reporters. No doubt no mere coincidence, the protest came off in some media sources as antiwomen—as if they were indicting the contestants—but the true goal was to protest the event itself. Nevertheless, the Miss America Pageant Protest put women's liberation on the national map, as it brought the topic to the national forefront, causing both the media and the public to pay attention. The media coverage drew more members to the NYRW afterwards, ironically widening the faction between politicos and feminists that ultimately doomed the NYRW.

An Antagonistic Interview on the David Susskind Show

The notoriety of the radical feminist movement skyrocketed even higher with a very special episode of the David Susskind Show in 1968 at WNTA-TV studios in New York City. Susskind had hosted a talk show on this station since 1958, interviewing such notable figures as Harry Truman and Nikita Khrushchev. On this particular day, however, Susskind had invited Rosalyn Baxandall, Kate Millett, Anselma Del'Olio, and Jacqui Ceballos to the studio. The host wanted to interview four women from the women's movement, and he reportedly told them candidly that they were chosen because they looked good. Susskind tried to refuse to allow a studio audience for this show, but reportedly gave in after a protest.

He immediately intensified the drama of the interview with the opening remark, "You are all so beautiful. What are you interested in Women's Liberation for?" (Ceballos 1991, 31). By the end of the show, he reportedly told them, "Who would want anyone like you all" (Ceballos 1991, 31). At one point Kate Millett responded, "What you need is a maid with bedroom privileges" (Ceballos 1991, 35), a statement considered scandalous at the time.

At one point Susskind said something about women being oppressed by the Miss America Contest, to which Baxandall replied: "Women are oppressed every day in their life. It's not only the Miss America Contest. Every day we go out; we have to put on make-up. We have to do this. We're oppressed by everything" (Ceballos 1991, 35).

The show was broadcast on a Sunday evening and syndicated around the nation, drawing numerous supportive letters and generating even greater interest in the women's movement.

Betty Friedan Versus Roxanne Dunbar

September of 1968 also brought to television another debate between personifications of the liberal and radical segments of the feminist movement. NOW's Betty Friedan and Roxanne Dunbar of Boston's

Cell 16 met a local television station in New York City (Dunbar could not recall which one). Dunbar showed up to the studio in militant garb, complete with white cotton sailor pants and white men's shirt. Friedan reportedly tried to get Dunbar in makeup, an exercise in futility from the outset. Among the two most outspoken figures in the women's movement, Friedan told Dunbar it was "scruffy feminists" that gave women's liberation a bad name, and she wanted no unity with radical feminists. Dunbar rebuked Friedan, telling her she feared losing her celebrity leadership position to a movement of women committed to collective action without leaders. Friedan called Dunbar an anarchist, to which Dunbar only agreed. The NOW president reportedly screamed as she stormed out of the studio. Later, Dunbar would question the viability of utilizing TV to promote the movement if it meant pitting one feminist against the other.

Feminists Protest the Nixon Inauguration

A rift between the women's movement and the New Left had already been evident, but it intensified at the January 22, 1969 Counter-Inaugural Demonstration, protesting the inauguration of Richard Nixon as the 37th President of the United States.

The event was organized by MOBE, the national Mobilization Committee to End the War in Vietnam. It was attended by such prominent feminist personalities as Shulamith Firestone, Ellen Willis, Irene Peslikis, Barbara Mehrof, Rosalyn Baxadall, Barbara Kamisky, and Sheila Cronan (author of the essay "Marriage"). The event furthered the division between the New York feminists and politicos from DC Women's Liberation, which allied with the New Left while it tried to encompass elements of politicos and feminists.

Marilyn Webb, founder of the politico DC Women's Liberation, took great pains in her speech not to criticize movement men. The same was not true of Shulamith Firestone, who virtually excoriated the men, and belittled the politicos' explanation that the oppression of women was due completely to capitalism. She accused the men of the Left of using the "revolution" merely as a means to grab personal power.

Women organizers intended to burn voter cards in protest against the incoming Nixon administration, the way the men would burn their draft cards. But as the mostly New Left crowd grew increasingly hostile toward the women's libbers, the destruction of voter cards fizzled amid the pandemonium. Baxandall recalled:

> It was huge, there were thousands. We insisted that a woman speak on the platform, and Shulie (Firestone) spoke. Men started yelling "Take her off the stage and fuck her." I mean, that was in 1968. Then they came to the platform to take her off, and the platform started sinking. Dave Dellinger said, "Please leave the platform," because it was such a hazard (Ceballos 1991, 16).

Protests 1969

Inspired by the guerilla street theater tactics of groups like WITCH, a group of Chicago women held a demonstration on January 16, 1969, in which they put a hex on the Sociology Department of the University of Chicago for firing the controversial Marxist feminist professor Marlene Dixon. Dixon had made several controversial proclamations to her students, including statements about how marriage perpetuates the oppression of women. Dixon's removal from the sociology faculty spurred numerous sit-ins by faculty and students alike. Her passionate publications in the 1960s and 1970s (e.g., *Things Which Are Done in Secret*) helped provide an academic validity for the spread of the radical feminist movement. She had been driven from the university presumably for her socialist affiliations. Dixon would go on to found Democratic Workers Party in California.

The Redstockings Stage a Speak-Out on Abortion

By 1969, many states had begun to look at reform of abortion laws, but many still utilized the formation of "therapeutic abortion committees" to determine the "worthiness" of the abortion. On February 13, 1969, the state of New York convened the Joint Legislative Committee on the Problems of Public Health for a hearing on possible changes in the 86-year-old law that criminalized abortion. The hearing panel included 12 men—professors, doctors, lawyers, and legislators—and a nun, but no women who had actually had experience with abortions.

One judge on the panel decided a particular woman could have an abortion because she "did her duty" of having four children prior. The radical group called the Redstockings picketed the committee, as Kathie Amatniek (Sarachild) stood up and advocated for repeal of all abortion laws. The hearing was disrupted, and had to be reconvened in another venue.

Eight days later, on Friday night, March 21, the Redstockings hosted their own hearing, which they called "Speak-out on Abortion." Held at Washington Square in Manhattan, the event was billed as a counterpoint to the state hearing on abortion, featuring 12 women who told of their own experiences concerning abortion. Amatniek, Rosalyn Baxandall, Robin Morgan, Lucinda Cisler, Irene Peslikis, and Barbara Mehrhof were among the women who spoke out and shared their experiences of abortions. The purpose of the Speak-Out was to raise "anger, empathy, pain" for the three hundred spectators who observed.

In the Speak-Out, one woman's story discussed the clandestine, criminal aspects of getting an abortion. Another woman described how her doctor would not authorize a "therapeutic abortion" unless she agreed—at the age of 20—to become sterilized. A third woman told of how a psychiatrist agreed to write a report attesting to her mental instability and need for an abortion—but only after she paid the all-important $60 fee. Another story was critical of the state panel of men and nun as nonexperts, while another described abortion as a relatively simple procedure made difficult by the stigma and perception of it. It's not the procedure, she said, but how women are made to feel about the procedure. At least two women commented on how this stigma can bring about suicidal thoughts.

Abortion became one of the first issues addressed by the newly formed Redstockings, and one of the few issues most radical feminists could agree upon. Redstockings member Lucinda "Cindy" Cisler led the charge for repeal of all abortion laws, claiming that abortion should be the right of every woman because it concerns her own body. Cisler published *Abortion Law Repeal: (sort of) a Warning to Women* which challenged the current laws concerning the performance of, consent for, and entitlement to abortion. Cisler would go on to serve as cochair of NOW's task force on abortion.

The Women's Movement Leaves the New Left Behind

By 1969, the women's movement had already begun to eclipse the New Left in terms of the lasting effect on the American psyche. In June of that year, the SDS held their last national convention in Chicago. The hangers-on of the waning New Left organization had tried to convince women their liberation was a part of the greater fight against capitalism, and that socialism would free women from chauvinism. However, the women and their supporters reiterated that all women suffer under the notion of male supremacy. A resolution presented to the gathered men—which included a statement of support for women's lib—was defeated. The separation of the women's movement from the Left—which began five years previously—was now all but complete.

By this time, the SDS had been taken over and factionalized by the Revolutionary Youth Movement, better known as the Weathermen. The Weatherman emphasized a more revolutionary, militaristic, and violent approach to the overthrow of the capitalistic system. The SDS underestimated and failed to include the middle class, imploding over militant self interest that negated the community interest.

In September of 1969, some of the leading figures of the New Left were put on trial before the national audience. Tried on charges of conspiracy to incite a riot at the 1968 Democratic National Convention, the "Chicago" Eight included SDS members David Dellinger, Tom Hayden, Rennie Davis, John Froines, and Lee Weiner; Yippies Jerry Rubin and Abbie Hoffman; and Black Panther Bobbie Seal, who was eventually severed from the trial and jailed for contempt. Fraught with showboat tactics by the defendants and judicial overreactions by Judge Julius Hoffman, the trial ended in a guilty verdict for Dellinger, Hayden, Davis, Froines, and Weiner. However, the convictions would be reversed by the Seventh Circuit Court of Appeals in 1972 because Judge Hoffman failed to allow inquiry into the potential cultural biases of the jury.

Finally, the disintegration of the New Left accelerated in October 1969, during the so called Days of Rage. Three hundred Weathermen engaged the Chicago Police in retaliation for the debacle during the August 1968 riot surrounding the Democratic Convention. In an attempt to bring the war home, more than two hundred Weathermen were arrested, severely crippling their numbers. The Weathermen erroneously assumed violence would lead to revolution, and that most people would join their side. But again, the Weathermen were severely mistaken in their assessment of the American middle class, which had yet to be jolted out of its complacency enough to support the overthrow of the American capitalistic system.

As the New Left continued to crumble, many more women turned their efforts to towards the separate women's liberation movement. Although some of the radical women did not object to violence per se, they abandoned the notion of machismo violence, which had increased under the direction of the Weathermen. In the end, the men of the New Left resisted real day-to-day change, like helping with housework, and giving up their male privileges. They mistakenly clung to the belief that feminism could expand the movement and would not contradict it. But the women had decided they could no longer be handcuffed by the men's resistance.

On September 23, 1969, The Feminists led a demonstration at the New York City Marriage License Board. Just before noon, Ti-Grace Atkinson, Pam Kearon, Sheila Cronan, Linda Feldman, and Marcia Winslow marched into the Municipal Building, surrounded by a phalanx of media. The Feminists had come to condemn a system in which, as Atkinson put it, "Marriage means rape and lifelong slavery . . . sex is overrated. If someday we have to choose between sex and freedom, there's no question I'd take freedom." The protesters claimed that all marriage was a fraud, and a form of slavery which systematically legitimized rape. They targeted Mayor John Lindsay—a father of four—as the "official representative of male society," and handed him a list of grievances. They disparaged consciousness-raising, claiming that sex roles—and the question of who is in control—were the basic problem that inflicted women in society. The protesters advocated for the annihilation of sex roles, claiming that men oppress women for psychological needs.

By this time, Ti-Grace Atkinson had become increasingly concerned with the image of radical feminists. She believed that women who associated with men undermined the movement. Atkinson said that husbands should pay for all labor in the house, and asserted that marriage means rape and lifelong slavery. In fact, she denounced all relationships with men, compared sex to mass psychosis, and characterized pregnancy as " . . . very painful. It's so immature to grow babies inside people's bodies. If we had test-tube babies, there would be less chance of deformed fetuses" (Davidson 1969, 2).

The First Congress to Unite Women, 1969

In November 1969 the first Congress to Unite Women was held in New York City. Boston's Cell 16 caused an uproar during a demonstration designed as a repudiation for the male idea of feminine superiority. Dana Densmore remembers:

> We were speaking from the stage on the subject of the political implications of our making ourselves into conventional womanly women through the cultivation (often at the expense of great time and effort) of stereotypical feminine appearance. To dramatize this, we included a bit of guerilla theater: one of our number (Martha Atkins) who had luxuriant long blonde hair had decided to cut it to a more practical chin length. To help us make the point about femininity, she had also agreed to have us cut her hair on stage. Jeanne Lafferty cut it. There was pandemonium in the hall, with women standing up and screaming, "don't do it!" One woman shrieked, "Men like my breasts, too; do you want me to cut them off?" (Densmore 1998, 84–85).

Under the campaign of Cell 16, sex was considered a conditioned need, only appropriate for reproduction. Densmore would say healthy people don't like being touched, and considered physical pleasure more of an issue for men than women. In something of a paradox, Cell 16 advocated for the elimination of sex, but also said maternalism was the cornerstone of the female principle, which all people must develop.

Women and Media

The Chicago Women's Liberation Rock Band

By 1970, women's liberation had become a well-known topic, and radical feminists looked for new ways to spread the message. In March of 1970, Naomi Weisstein led the first performance of the Chicago's

Women's Liberation Rock Band. The band featured Sherry Jenkins on voice and lead guitar, Pat Solo on rhythm guitar, Susan Abod playing bass, Sanya Montalvo and Susan Prescott on drums, with Weisstein on piano. They performed songs such as "Secretary" and "Mountain Moving Day" and "Poppa Don't Lay That Shit on Me", at venues that included the Second Annual Third World Transvestite Ball, the University of Pittsburgh, and Cornell University with New Haven Women's Liberation Rock Band. Chicago Women's Liberation Rock Band enjoyed remarkable success, presenting explicitly political performances which were highly interactive with both male and female audiences. They boosted an image of feminist solidarity, resistance, and power which the audiences loved.

> About one performance (University of Pittsburgh, 1971), Weisstein wrote
> "I went to imitate Mick Jagger singing" "Under My Thumb" "There is a squirrelly dog who once had her day ..." Then I asked the audience: "And do you know what he says then? He says, 'It's alright.'" Pause. "Well, it's not all right, Mick Jagger, and IT'S NEVER GOING TO BE ALL RIGHT AGAIN (cheers from the audience) IT'S NEVER GOING TO BE ALL RIGHT AGAIN!" The audience didn't stop screaming for five minutes (Weisstein 1998, 355).

Calling rock music "the insurgent culture of the era," the band disagreed with the New Left idea that by changing the political structures, change in consciousness would follow. According to Weisstein, the "idea of direct cultural intervention in order to change consciousness was held in low esteem by most of the CWLU leadership at the time." The Chicago Women's Liberation Rock Band actually recorded a record for Rounder Records in 1972. Within three years the band had broken up "in an agony of hatred and hidden agendas."

The *Ladies' Home Journal* Sit-In

On March 18, 1970, members of the Redstockings, the Feminists, and other groups joined in the *Ladies' Home Journal* Sit-in with the leadership of a group called Media Women. The Media Women were comprised of journalism professionals from the print, radio, and television

The Ladies' Home Journal *protest, March 18, 1970, New York City (Bettmann/CORBIS).*

media, including Lucy Komisar, Nora Ephron, and Susan Brownmiller. At the time, the *Ladies' Home Journal* had a paid circulation of more than six million, yet more than half of its articles were written by men. It also had a black readership of more than 1.2 million, but only one story in the last 12 months had been written by an African American. The magazine's slogan was "Never Underestimate the Power of a Woman"; hence, it seemed a perfect target at which to aim the issue of equal representation of women and people of color in journalism.

At about 9:15 a.m. more than one hundred women—surrounded by a horde of media—stormed the office of *Ladies' Home Journal* editor John Mack Carter. They presented a list of demands, including the replacement of the editorial staff and the advertising staff—including Carter—by women. The demonstrators insisted that Carter hire black staff in proportion to black readers. They also demanded an in-house daycare center and the elimination of ads demeaning to women. The protestors wanted the focus of articles to be on real issues for women, and they wanted the magazine to publish an article on the women's movement, penned by movement participants.

The scene within the editorial office grew increasingly fiery, until Shulamith Firestone jumped on a desk, started ripping up magazines, and reportedly even tried to lead an attack on Carter from the desk. The editor finally conceded to a meeting with a smaller group to negotiate the demands. In the end, only one of the demands was actually granted: an eight-page supplement on the women's liberation movement, penned by feminist writers, for 10 thousand dollars.

Many saw the *Ladies' Home Journal* Sit-in as a mere grab-for-glory by the writers associated with the movement. The event was criticized for giving up on the more radical—and important— demands. Others criticized Firestone for her violent outburst, saying her actions actually jeopardized the negotiations. In the end, the *Journal* may have been helped more than it was hurt, benefiting from the extra publicity.

In any case, the sit-in turned out to be the first of several media events that acknowledge the rise of the feminists. On March 19, 1970, 46 women staffers at *Newsweek* filed sex discrimination charges against the magazine. More women filed similar discrimination charges against *Time Magazine* and NBC.

The radical edge of the women's movement developed increasing hostility with the mainstream patriarchal and patronizing press.

> The Mass Media plays a crucial role in creating and perpetuating America's dominant ideology: racism, imperialism, chauvinism, authorianism . . . We have been brainwashed to believe that the American press is free; that it provides objective coverage of the news, all the news, and that it is a public service . . . The press is basically a voice for the ruling class (McEldowney and Poole 1970, 40).

Radical feminists refused to speak with male reporters while bringing more pressure upon the media to hire women, who hopefully would provide more thorough, unbiased coverage of women's issues.

The "Lavender Menace" Is Introduced

On May 1, 1970, at Intermediate School 70 in the Chelsea neighborhood of Manhattan, more than three hundred women awaited the opening ceremonies of the 2nd Congress to Unite Women. At

7:15 p.m., the auditorium suddenly went dark. The sounds of running and a rebel yell preceded the lights returning. Forty women—including Artemis March, Rita Mae Brown, Cynthia Funk, Martha Shelley, March Hoffman, Lois Hart, Kate Millett, and Ellen Bedoz—had taken over the assembly. Identifying themselves as Radicalesbians, 17 of them—adorned in lavender T-shirts with the words "Lavender Menace" stenciled on front—commandeered the stage, inviting other women to join them. With the second congress clearly in their hands, the lavender menace protesters held sway over the convention, talking for two hours of the hazards of a lesbian lifestyle in a heterosexual, homophobic culture.

By the end of the convention the assembly had adopted a series of resolutions. The resolutions sought to dispel the notion that women's liberation was simply a lesbian plot, and urged that the lesbian label be used in a positive light. They proposed that homosexuality is a viable means of birth control, and that sex education should include the subject of lesbianism. The resolutions challenged the gathering fears about lesbians, and suggested that lesbianism provided a means of liberation from male-dominated heterosexuality. They proposed that lesbianism could be thought of as the quintessential act of political solidarity among women.

The Women's Strike for Equality

On August 26, 1970, the 50th Anniversary of the ratification of the 19th Amendment, NOW sponsored the Women's Strike for Equality in New York City, and in 90 other towns and cities in 40 states. Between 35 thousand and 75 thousand demonstrators participated around the county, making it the largest demonstration for women's rights in American history. Women demanded equal opportunities in employment and education, and unfettered access to abortion and child care. The event helped bring women's liberation further to the forefront of American consciousness, and helped raise consciousness of the unappreciated role of women in society.

Women's March for Equality, Detroit Contingency, August 26, 1970 (© Bettmann/CORBIS).

Protests against Rape

On January 24, 1971, the NYRF held its Speak Out on rape at St. Clement's Episcopal Church on W. 46th Street in New York. Similar to the Redstocking's Speak Out on abortion the previous year, the NYRF invited women who had been raped to speak out, and 10 turned up to do just that. Admission was free to women, but men were charged two dollars. More than three hundred attendees (15 of whom were men) filled the auditorium, with standing room only.

Among those who spoke out, one woman talked about being raped 15 years earlier by four men. Another woman described the childhood ritual of "pants-ing" by a pack of neighborhood boys. A third woman talked about being raped by a medical student, while another revealed that she had been raped by her therapist. They also discussed the ramifications for the victim, as well as the unsupportive reactions from family members, boyfriends, police, and others—who often (sometimes inadvertently) blamed the victim.

On April 17, 1971, a conference on rape at Washington Irving High School further raised consciousness on issue. All the while, Susan Brownmiller gathered information, impressions, and inspirations for the 1975 release of the definitive *Against Our Will.*

Works Cited

American Experience, People & Events: The 1968 Protest, 1999–2001, www.pbs.org/wgbh.amex/missamerica/peopleevents/e_feminists.html.

Ceballos, Jacqueline Michot, Interview with Rosalyn Baxandallo, The Radcliffe Institute for Advanced Study, Cambridge, 1991, 16, 31, 35.

Davidson, Sara, An Oppressed Majority Demands Its Rights, *Life Magazine*, 1969, 2. Densmore, Dana, *A Year of Living Dangerously, Feminist Memoir Project, Voices from Women's Liberation*, New York: Three Rivers Press (Crown Publishers) 1998, 84–85.

Dunbar, Roxanne, "Outlaw Woman: Chapters from a Feminist Memoir in Progress," *The Feminist Memoir Project: Voices from Women's Liberation*, 1998, New York: Three Rivers Pres, New York, 93.

Firestone, Shulameth, "The Jeanette Rankin Brigade: Woman Power? A Summary of our Involvement," *Notes from the First Year*, June 1968.

Freeman, Jo, W.I.T.C.H.—The Women's International Conspiracy from Hell, 2009, http://www.jofreeman.com/photos/witch.html.

Hanisch, Carol, "The 1968 Miss America Protest," *The Feminist Memoir Project: Voices from Women's Liberation*, 1998, New York: Three Rivers Press, 197–8.

McEldowney, Carole, and Poole, Rosemary, "A Working Paper on the Media," Women: A Journal of Liberation, Spring 1970, 40.

Weisstein, Naomi, "Days of Celebration and Resistance," *The Feminist Memoir Project: Voices from Women's Liberation*, 1998, New York: Three Rivers Press, 351, 355.

CHAPTER FOUR

Key Issues of the Movement

Although the list of social and political issues for which the radical feminists fought was vast and varied, the most important ones can be divided into two categories: control over the body, and pursuit of equal opportunity.

Control over the Body

Abortion

In no other forum of debate can the power struggle over the control over women's bodies be more dramatically witnessed than around the issue of abortion. The abortion issue raised questions of self-determination and equality, and the right to control fertility. It pitted a woman's right to privacy and control over her own self against the government which, of course, was dominated by men.

By the time of the Redstockings' Speak Out on Abortion in 1969, many states had begun to look at reforms in the abortion laws, but many still clung to the concept of "therapeutic abortion." The definition of "therapeutic"—which encompasses life, health, economic, and psychological factors—was often determined in committees convened to determine the "worthiness" of the abortion.

In 1969, Lucinda "Cindy" Cisler led the charge for repeal of all abortion laws, and the recognition that abortion is the right of every woman because it ultimately concerns her body. Cisler published "Abortion Law Repeal (sort of): A Warning to Women" in the newsletter *Notes from the Second Year*. In it, she vigorously proposed reform measures as counterpoints to the regulations and thinking of the day. She advocated for the performance of abortions at legal outpatient clinics, which negated the need for licensed hospitals, further simplifying an already normally simple procedure.

Cisler pointed out that childbirth can be many times more dangerous than an abortion, and the perceived need of a licensed physician not only made the procedure less accessible, but also more expensive. She argued against the stance that an abortion could not be administered beyond a certain time in pregnancy, which ultimately took the choice away from women. Cisler argued that a woman belonged to herself and not to the state, and that the final decision must rest with her. Finally, she drew attention to the dangers facing wives or pregnant teens, who must obtain spousal or parental consent. Again, such regulations take away the control a woman has over her own body, and may make the situation worse by involving abusive or neglectful parties.

Because of the complications surrounding access to safe abortions, many communities found ways of providing abortions in a clandestine manner. The most famous such service was JANE, begun in Chicago in 1967. It started as an informal program which referred women by word of mouth to physicians willing to provide "The Service." JANE eventually facilitated as many as one hundred illegal abortions per week—many administered safely without medical personnel at all. Women were willing to cross over the law in order to obtain an abortion quickly, with a minimum of complications—something they would not get if they sought a legal abortion.

Of course a woman was lucky if she was able to find a competent doctor willing to provide an abortion. The provision of unsafe, "back-alley" abortions remained a significant public health problem. Doctors willing to provide an abortion as responsible medical care faced a myriad of sanctions and admonitions. The importance of access to abortion was underscored by the sorrow of unwanted children and unhappy families, let alone the global issue of over-population. The triad of risk in abortions was often presented as protection of women versus protection of doctors versus protection of the unborn.

With the 1973 decision in *Roe v. Wade*, the Supreme Court determined that it was a woman's constitutional right to have an abortion within the first trimester of a pregnancy. Although the decision did not in any way address the question of when life began, antiabortion arguments shifted to the viability of the fetus, rather the rights of the woman over her body:

> ... the charge of baby killing was also potent code for male-supremacists worse nightmare: women cut loose from their anatomical destiny; women putting their needs and desires before their age-old obligation to create and nurture new life; women having sex on their own terms and without fear; women becoming players on the world stage instead of providing the back drop—and the safety net—for men. On the deepest level, the right to life movement spoke to the primal fears that if women stop subordinating themselves to their role as caretakers of men and children, civilization and morality as we know them will give way to destruction and chaos (Echols 1989, viii).

After *Roe v. Wade*, the conservative, antiabortion contingent asserted that abortion takes a life created at contraception, undermines traditional family roles, and allows women to be as promiscuous as men. Antiabortion forces, such as Senator Henry Hyde (R-Illinois), stepped up their efforts to limit access to the procedure. In 1976 Congress passed the Hyde Amendment, which decreased availability of contraceptives and birth control procedures to poor women by making federal Medicaid funds less available to pay for them. Opponents of the amendment said it was indicative of the antichoice movement growing among conservatives. Amendment opponents pointed to women such as Rose Jimenez, who died from an infection she contracted undergoing an illegal abortion. She chose an illegal abortion because her Medicaid would not pay for the abortion. The case of Rosa Jimenez would be cited for those urging the repeal of the Hyde

Amendment, demonstrating that women will seek out abortions illegally if the procedure is not available to them.

> Hidden from the debate on abortion in the funding cases was an issue that had been part of the abortion law reform movement from its inception in the 1930s: the rich could afford to find and finance abortions; the poor could not. The poor would have their children and get poorer, or seek and sometimes die from illegal abortions or self-inflicted abortions (Hull and Hoffer 2001, 201).

Even as late as 2010, however, the antiabortion forces would rally to block federal dollars for abortion from President Barack Obama's efforts toward health care reform.

The amendment of abortion laws and attitudes was perhaps the first major public policy effect of the radical feminist movement.

The movement's demand for repeal laws spurred the general acceleration in the abortion campaign and its influence. As women are still facing reform measures that merely add abortion laws, the radical feminist position is that what is needed is not more abortion laws, but the recognition that it is not for the government to decide what a woman should do with her body, but rather it is for the individual woman.

Rape

Kate Millett in *Sexual Politics* (1968) asserted that women have learned to accept the subordinate position in society, that rape was a weapon for the patriarchy, and sex itself was a tool for dominance and oppression. In 1975, Susan Brownmiller described rape as nothing more or less than a conscious process of intimidation by which all men keep all women in a state of fear. She wrote:

> Rape has been not only a male prerogative, but man's basic weapon of fear against women (Brownmiller, 2009).

Brownmiller's definitive treatise on the subject of rape was called *Against Our Will: Men, Women, & Rape. Against Our Will* became a comprehensive study of rape as a means of fear and control.

Brownmiller examines the criminal rapist, the strange lone predator against the female victim. She also studies the incidents of interracial rape, and how the fear of such acts fueled the white man's brutality against the black man. She additionally reveals historically how men have used rape in wartime as a sign of complete domination, and intimidation of the conquered society—both men and women. Rape has been used by conquering armies to completely subdue the enemy, taking control of all of his "possessions," including women—which for centuries is how they have been regarded.

But Brownmiller—and many other radical feminists—took the discussion of rape a step further. According to Brownmiller, marriage was an institution for the license of rape, and a societal means to keep women subordinate to men. She discussed how historically rape was considered not possible within a marriage, since it was assumed in marriage a woman gave consent to sex—apparently at any given moment. In the 1969 Feminists demonstration at the New York City Marriage License Board, they claimed that all marriage was a fraud, and a form of slavery which systematically legitimized rape.

Brownmiller also highlighted the cultural tendency to disbelieve a woman who cried "rape," whether within the marriage or without. She explored the myths that surrounded the rape, such as the "female tendency to lie" or the belief that "no woman can be raped against her will."

The power of the book was the scope by which the subject was addressed, a subject that had previously rarely been examined, and certainly not to this degree. As with much of the literature of the radical feminists, the potency lies in tackling the subject for the first time. Although there may have been some discrepancies—and some claimed the book was too graphic—perhaps Brownmiller was trying to make up for lost time by exploring as many aspects of the subject as possible.

The radical feminists' efforts to focus attention on rape has paid dividends over time. Awareness and laws concerning rape and domestic violence have greatly increased since the 1970s. Rape Crisis and Domestic Violence Centers are now staple institutions in society, and much has been accomplished to change public opinion and revise laws on sexual assault. Health collectives featuring women physicians and clinicians offer alternatives to male-dominated medicine and the lack of sensitivity to these topics. Law enforcement has also been sensitized to see domestic violence and rape as public health and criminal matters, not just hidden domestic issues. Events such as the "Take Back the Night" march—initiated in November 1978, and intended to raise awareness of rape and date rape—have raised awareness to stop blaming the victim. Legislation such as the Violence Against Women Act was passed in 1999, paving the way for legal, law enforcement, educational, and social service responses to acts of violence against women.

The radical feminist position juts up against a conservative response—and also a younger generation's response—to the issue of rape. In Katie Roiphe's *The Morning After: Sex, Fear, and Feminism on Campus* (1993), the author explores what she calls rape hysteria. She suggests how rape hype betrays feminism and undermines the power and responsibility of women. She asserts that this culture of fear oppresses women as much as the past culture of dependence. She asserts that women are not passive and helpless victims, not frail flowers and perpetual targets. She states that the modern woman debunks helplessness, which she thinks rape hysteria undermines.

Celibacy

Several segments of the radical feminists came to the conclusion that heterosexual sex—the need for intercourse—merely reassures supremacy for men, who fear sexual irrelevance. But radical feminists claim vaginal intercourse is unneeded for a woman and does little for her; in fact autosexuality is all that is required for the sexual urge. Kate Millett considered the celibate to be the most lucid person, stating that sex is a minor need blown out of proportion by men. Many advocated lesbianism as separation from men both personally and politically. In *The SCUM Manifesto*, Valerie Solanas wrote:

> The female can easily—far more easily than she may think—condition away her sex drive, leaving her completely cool and cerebral and free to pursue truly worthy relationships and activities . . . sex is the refuge of the mindless (Solanas 1967, 10).

In The *Myth of Vaginal Orgasm*, Ann Koedt asserted that even sexual intercourse was an oppressive act, because it focused on the needs and wants of the male, and not the female. Radical feminists determined that the sex need is a delusion, perpetuated by the patriarchy as another way to keep women subservient to men. They asserted that women should be liberated from heterosexual sex—and all forms of dependence on men.

Contraception

In June of 1965, in the case of *Griswold v. Connecticut*, the United State Supreme Court overturned the conviction of Estelle T. Griswold, Executive Director, of the New Haven office of Planned Parenthood. Griswold had been charged with the crime of giving contraceptive information to married couples. But the court declared Connecticut's law unconstitutional, as a violation of the right to privacy.

In writing the 6–2 decision, Justice William O. Douglas declared:

> We deal with the right of privacy older than the Bill of Rights— older than our political parties, older than our school system. Marriage is a coming together, for better or worse, hopefully enduring, and intimate to the degree of being sacred. It is an association that promotes a way of life, not causes; a harmony of living, not political faith; bilateral loyalty not commercial or social projects (Griswold v. Connecticut, 1965).
>
> ... although right to marital privacy is not explicitly protected by Constitution, it fell under the "penumbra" of fundamental constitutional guarantees of freedom of association, privacy of the home, protection against self incrimination, and due process (Kohn 1991, 143).

After the United States Food and Drug Administration authorized the sale of the combined oral contraceptive Enovid in 1960, women suddenly gained more control of their own bodies and reproduction than any time previous in history. The availability of oral contraception meant that women could readily be sexually active without risking pregnancy, greatly decreasing their dependence on men. Within three years, more than 2.3 million women were using it, and by 1963, one out of every four women under the age of 45 in the United States had used the pill. Within a decade, more than 50 million women would use it throughout the world; by 1990, 60 million, revolutionizing planned contraception on a global scale.

The radical feminists whole-heartedly continued the 50-year old legacy of Margaret Sanger—who was arrested for opening the first birth control clinic in New York in 1916. For the feminists, the access to contraceptive information, practices, and devices was just another aspect of recognizing the complete control that women should have over their own bodies. Although not as volatile a subject as abortion, the advocacy for easy access to birth control was another way of combating the conservative, male-dominated efforts to keep women "barefoot and pregnant" in their maternal and domestic roles. Those conservative forces argued that the unrestricted use of contraceptives devalued family values, threatened the institution of marriage, and supported the promiscuity of women (as much as men, evidently). In reality, from the radical feminist point of view, contraception (as well as abortion) gave control of fertility to women, where it rightfully belonged. As Alan Guttmacher, former president of Planned Parenthood, wrote:

> No woman is completely free unless she is wholly capable of controlling her fertility and . . . no baby receives its full birthright unless it is born gleefully wanted by its parents (Guttmacher 2008).

Through publications such as the Boston's Women's Health Collective's *Our Bodies, Ourselves*, and through organizations such as Planned Parenthood, radical feminists sought to bring contraceptive and reproductive information to women on a mass scale. The radical feminists challenged the fear, apathy, and ignorance of the patriarchal society by raising these important health and social issues of women in a way that had never been done before.

Pornography

The debate over pornography pitted feminists who saw it as an illustration of the violent and demeaning attitude towards sex supported by the patriarchal society, and those who defended an individual's right to choose the means of sexual expression. Robin Morgan defined pornography as the theory for which rape was the practice, as the ultimate form of oppression of females. According to radical feminists, pornography illustrated male power over women in its most graphic form, and also illustrated how the male concept or principle created the chaotic, violent, greedy world, antithetical to the female principle. For the radical feminists, women became involved in pornography for the same reasons they fell into prostitution: because of the image that the patriarchy imposed upon them, and because of the lack of economic opportunities for women. They believed that women's behavior was due to sexual conditioning and collaboration with the oppressive system. Dana Densmore said women must be conditioned to stop believing in their own inferiority.

In 1979, several names from the earlier part of the women's movement—including Susan Brownmiller, Robin Morgan, Gloria Steinham, Lois Gould, Andrea Dworkin, and Lynn Campbell—formed the organization Woman Against Pornography (WAP), headquartered at 579 Ninth Avenue near 42nd Street. In the heart of New York's sex industry, WAP became known for its tours of Times Square. Conducted on Sundays and Tuesday evenings, the tours introduced uninformed people to the violent nature of the four billion dollar pornography industry. The WAP activity culminated in October with a conference at Martin Luther King High School on October 16, 1979. The conference featured a Speak Out, in which women talked about the connection between pornography and their personal abuse

The Anti-Porn March, Times Square, New York City (© Bettmann/CORBIS).

as children. On the fourth day of the conference, WAP led a march of five thousand on Times Square.

The antiporn activity witnessed the unusual symbiosis of the antiporn feminists—who asserted the oppressive effect on men's attitudes—and antiporn conservatives, who wanted to control the proliferation of pornographic material in American society in the wake of the sexual revolution. This debate on pornography divided the feminist community, between those who wanted to protect an individual's right to choose what to read or view, versus the need to protect potential victims.

Prostitution

Like pornography, women's participation in prostitution was due largely to the dearth of opportunities available to women in the patriarchal society, as well as the oppressive and objectifying attitudes toward sex. Susan Brownmiller published "Speaking out on Prostitution" in the NYRW's *Notes from the Third Year* in 1971.

> So, now you can understand why I identify with the prostitute, and why, when I see a front page headline in the *New York Times*, "Mayor Stepping Up Drive on Prostitutes and Smut," I know that in a very real sense it is me and my entire sex that the mayor and the *New York Times* are talking about. And when this mayor appoints a task force of six men and no women to study the problems of pimps, pornography, and prostitution, giving equal moral weight to each category, I know that his failure to appoint even one woman to this task force is not an oversight, it's just that the boys decided they've got to get together and do a little superficial something to preserve their fun (Brownmiller 1971, 75).

Brownmiller identified prostitutes as victims, not merely businesswomen who had chosen a particular vocation. She argued that prostitution existed due to the very few career options available for women. She wrote:

> Prostitution will not end in this country until men see women as equals . . . so it seems that we will have to work for the full equality of women and the end of prostitution side by side (Brownmiller 1971).

In Bromberg's *Feminist Issues in Prostitution*, the author identified nine categories of prostitutes:

1. Fall into poverty, turn to prostitution until they find something else
2. Poor family with long history of poverty and lack of education
3. Abducted and forced against will
4. Volunteers due to defects in moral character
5. Distanced and demoralized as children, could not get sufficient attention
6. Low intelligence, physical and mental disabilities
7. A fish to water, cater to high priced clients (Bromberg 1997)

In December of 1971, the NYRF and The Feminists held a conference on prostitution at Charles Evans Hughes High School in New York. The keynote speaker was feminist theologian Mary Daly from Boston. The conference seemed to many more like social work than feminism. While the organizers discussed the issue of prostitution from the economic oppression standpoint, several prostitutes in the audience challenged the notion that prostitution exploited women's bodies any more than low-paying, hard physical labor exploited men's bodies. They objected to the feminists' statements, apparently taking it as criticism of them, rather than the economic environment that fostered their profession. The arguing became enflamed, and a scuffle broke out among the women. As Susan Brownmiller described, "That ended our campaign to eliminate prostitution" (Brownmiller 1971, 75).

Equal Opportunity

The other category of issues that concerned the radical feminists involved equal opportunity. The primary reason that the feminists broke away from the male New Left in the first place was because of the lack of equal opportunity within the movement. Providing this equal opportunity meant not only persuading the patriarchy to allow women to pursue whatever vocation they wanted but also helping women to understand that they were capable of pursuing those vocations. Meredith Tax wrote:

> We have to try to imagine what we could have been if we hadn't been taught from birth that we are stupid, unable to analyze

anything, "intuitive", passive, physically weak, hysterical, overemotional, dependent by nature, incapable of defending ourselves against any attack, fit only to be a housekeeper, sex object, and emotional service center for some man, or men, and children (Tax 1969, 4).

The radical feminists urged women to let go of the fear that they were nothing apart from men and children, and that they were intelligent, competent individuals in their own right, with the ability and the right to pursue any avenue in life they deemed appropriate. The radical women campaigned that, in subordinating their ambition for the sake of their husbands and children, girls had been deprived of their own ego and own sense of self. Girls had been stupefied at adolescence with social pressure, relegating their own aspirations in support of those who will be their intimates—namely, men and children (particularly boys).

The radical feminists also believed child care to be one of the great obstacles blocking women from pursuing equal opportunities in life and work. Women were expected to set aside their own personal goals and dreams when children appeared within the family, and take on the role of housekeeper and child raiser while men pursued their personal ambitions in the guise of providing for the family. From early on, organizations such as NYRW worked to make affordable, community child care available to women, so that they might—at least on some level—be able to raise children and pursue their own professional lives.

> ... the substantive equality radical feminists demanded: the idea that men could share housework and child rearing is not real to her, and so special treatment seems to her the only alternative to the present untenable situation. She does not recognize that before feminism, her career-minded family would probably have been resolved before it started—by job discrimination and social pressures on mothers to stay home. Nor does she see that her indignant, unquestioned sense of her right to combine child rearing and other work without unreasoned sacrifice is the product of the anti-sexist values the movement fought for. Nor does she know that many of her arguments against this culture's pervasive anti-mother bias were first made by radical feminists, who pointed out the hypocrisy of a society that sentimentalizes motherhood while devaluing the work that mothers do; who called attention to the "working mother" (and

coined the phrase "every mother is a working mother"); who decried the double bind faced by women who want children, but also want, as men do, to be out in the public world (Echols 1989, xiv).

Firestone and others took the issue further, advocating the dissipation of the nuclear family—seen as the heart of the tyranny against women—in favor of community units, where children would be raised virtually "by the village." Not only would the commune free women to pursue their own professional interests, but because they were raised by both men and women in the community setting, girls would not be pigeonholed into particular roles and tasks that would dominate their lives. They would be shielded from the sexist and repressive modes of traditional family life. Firestone advocated free and unrestricted access to both contraception and government-sponsored child care, to allow women as much control as possible over their reproductive and domestic activities.

In their campaigns for child care and equal opportunity, the radical feminists ran up against the right wing's protection of "the sanctity of the family." In December of 1971, for example, Congress passed the Comprehensive Child Development Act, which provided $2 million annually toward a national day care system, which would free more women to pursue careers. However, the act was vetoed by Republican President Richard Nixon, for fear that such a program would be deemed communistic.

More Opportunities for Women

Whereas radical feminism sought to change the structure of the society, and liberal feminism looked at reforming the precepts of society, cultural feminism pursued the creation of a separate society, one in which women were availed every opportunity in a culture which paralleled the dominant patriarchy of mainstream America. Whereas radical feminism confronted the political and social structures, cultural feminism emphasized developing the personal despite the influence of those structures.

Cultural feminism witnessed the development of female business, such as health centers, credit unions, rape crisis centers, bookstores, presses, and other enterprises directed and managed by women. The idea was that if the patriarchal culture would not support female entrepreneurs, women would create a culture in which they could rise and flourish.

> ... most fundamentally, radical feminism was a political movement dedicated to eliminating the sex-class system ... cultural feminism was a counterculture movement aimed at reversing the cultural valuation of the male and the devaluation of the female ...
>
> In the terminology of today, radical feminists were typically social constructionists who wanted to render gender irrelevant, while cultural feminists were generally essentialists who sought to celebrate femaleness.... Thus, we find radical feminists mobilizing women on the basis of their similarity to men, and cultural feminists organizing women around the principle of female difference (Echols 1989, 6).

The Furies and other organizations created such female institutions that would employ feminists and keep opportunities open for women only. Some of these enterprises included publisher Diana Press (Coletta Reid), recording distributor Olivia Records (Jennifer Woodul), Women in Distribution, and *Quest,* a feminist quarterly journal. Female businesses put women in a position to gain and use economic power, but many of these companies only lasted a short while, and ended up benefiting only a small number of women. Critics of the feminist businesses alleged alternate businesses actually only benefitted the few white middle class women who had the resources to start them. Critics of cultural feminism stated that such pursuits created illusions of progress and success for a scant few, while doing nothing to alleviate the real menace—the mainstream patriarchal society which cut off opportunity for a vast number of women.

Some radical feminists targeted organized religion for not only supporting and preaching the maintenance of the patriarchal society, but for grossly limiting leadership opportunities for women within the religious organizations themselves, and thus within the larger society. Even in churches which proposed a liberal theology, opportunities for ministry leadership for women remained few through the radical feminist era. Women such as Sally Priesand—who in 1972 became the first woman rabbi in the United States—pioneered the then radical idea that Divinity could provide inspiration and spiritual intervention through women just as well as men. She felt the pressure and the discomfort from congregations trying to accept the concept of a female rabbi. Said Priesand, who served the community at Monmouth Reform Temple in Tinton Falls, New Jersey, "Though Reform Judaism had long before declared an official religious equality between men and women, Reform Jews still believed that a woman's place was in the home . . . they were not yet ready for the spiritual leadership of a woman" (Priesand 1996, xiii–xiv).

Through her career, Priesand remained a tireless reformer, nudging the antiquity of Judaism toward the full acceptance of women in its practice and community.

Mary Daly, a Boston College theologian who waged the educational war against the patriarchal religions, took the campaign much further. She declared the oppression of women had its roots in religious institutions. Daly condemned most of the world's religions as sanctifying the passivity of women with the promise of afterlife happiness. She indicated that organized patriarchal religions in general and the Roman Catholic Church in particular—for all its apparent compassion for equality and justice—continued to perpetuate the notion of the natural inferiority of women, and the oppression of women, by systematically keeping women from the leadership and decision-making roles within the institution. She concluded that all the major religions oppressed and objectifed women, and saw sexism in language as a stumbling block to explanation of female spirituality.

Then there have been those among the radical feminists who questioned the very compatibility of feminism and capitalism. The very notion of sexism is a social system:

> . . . embedded in law, tradition, economics, education, organized religion, science, language, the mass media, sexuality morality, child rearing, the domestic division of labor, and everyday social interaction.
>
> It is reinforced through social condemnation, ridicule, ostracism, sexual rejection and harassment, the withholding of birth control and abortion, economic deprivation, and male violence condoned by the state (Willis 1989, ix).

Conservatives often criticized radical feminist efforts to create equal opportunity for women as a subversion of traditional values and destabilization of the family. But radical feminists asserted that the patriarchal society used the myths of traditional family values to control women, limiting their opportunities in society. In 1971, Jo Freeman published "The Building of the Gilded Cage" in NYRW's *Notes from the Third Year*. The essay examined the historic social control which supported the perpetual tutelage of women, keeping women as perpetual children. The essay explored the *Patria potestus*, or power of the father, and the rights—or lack thereof—of women in marriage. She described how relinquishing one's name and taking the last name of one's husband created the loss of a woman's own separate identity.

The article also looked at the historic protection laws—such as illustrated in the Supreme Court case of *Muller v. Oregon*—limiting the hours of women in the workplace in the few jobs open for women. Freeman asserted that paternalism took the disguise of "protection" and "privilege", while corporations and male-run unions took advantage of protection laws to limit women as competition for working men. Freeman wrote how most women thoroughly internalized the social division, and refused to recognize the oppression. She recognized socialization as the most insidious form of social control, writing, "No group is so oppressed as one which will not recognize its own oppression" (Freeman 1971, 139). In June of 1963, Congress passed the Equal Pay Act of 1963, which made it illegal to pay men and women different wage rates for equal work on jobs that require equal skill, effort, and responsibility, and are performed under similar work conditions. Yet disparities existed and continue to exist. At the time, women were earning 58 cents for every dollar men earned. Thirty-five years later in 2003, the Census Bureau revealed the wage gap had closed, but the discrepancy was still 75 cents for women for every dollar for men, with older women typically earning less than younger women (Berkeley 1999, 105).

Historically, there have been two theories concerning disparity in pay. The first, the choice theory, says that pay disparity exists due to different choices and values that men and women choose in their career—men routinely accept more dangerous and higher paying careers than women while women typically choose to devote a substantial amount of their career path time to families and parenting (also known as the "mommy track"). This is the position often taken by conservatives such as Kate O'Beirne, who wrote:

Disparities in wages largely exist between women with children, and men and single women. This is not sex discrimination, but rather the result of choices mothers freely make in their desire to balance work and family responsibilities (O'Beirne 2006, 48).

The second theory is the discrimination theory, espoused by the Equal Opportunity Commission. It states that the effects of continuing inequity are still experienced in the form of gender segregation in the work force, the undervaluation in the types of jobs held prevalently by women, inequities built into the pay system itself, and differences in work patterns.

In February of 1964, due to the efforts of representatives Martha Griffiths (D-MI) and Katherine St. George (R-NY), the "sex" amendment was added to Title VII of the Civil Rights Act of 1964, outlawing discrimination in voting, access to public education, employment, public accommodations, and federally assisted programs on the basis of race, ethnicity, religion, *or* sex. The action would come to be regarded as Ladies Day in the House. Yet Ladies Day did not last very long, as since that time opportunities in careers have remained skewed for men:

> Title VII defined this sex discrimination as well as other employment practices as discriminatory and therefore illegal, but until the five-person EEOC took its charge of enforcement seriously, the 4000 cases of sex discrimination filed by women workers between 1964 and 1966 were treated as frivolous complaints (Berkeley 1999, 28).

However, since the radical feminist era, the gap has closed considerably. Between 1970 and 1990, the percentage of women lawyers and judges rose from 5 to 24 percent; the percentage of physicians increased 9 to 21 percent; and accountants and auditors rose from 25 to 53 percent.

Even in more traditional female occupations, such as education, the disparities were obvious. In fact, the 1963 Equal Pay Act did not even include positions in education. In 1963, women made up only 13 percent of school principals, and 10 percent of full professors in colleges and universities. But into and beyond the radical feminist era, the increases could be seen as remarkable. In 1972, Title VII was revamped to include educational institutions. By 1970, the percentage of female professors had increased to 28 percent, and by 1990, 40 percent. The growth in opportunities for women could be measured simply in the number of women's studies courses that had emerged on American college campuses. In 1973 there were 2,000 such courses; by 1999 the number had increased to 30,000.

> Title VI sought to guard a woman's rights to choose her career path—despite perceived hazards or difficulties. Title VII rejects this type of romantic paternalism as unduly Victorian and instead vests individual women with the power to decide whether or not to take on unromantic tasks. Men have always had the right to determine whether the increase in remuneration for strenuous, dangerous, obnoxious, boring, or unromantic tasks is worth the candle. The promise of Title VII is that women are now to be on equal footing (Berkeley 1999, 60).

The Equal Employment Opportunity Commission (EEOC) was formed in 1965 to enforce the Civil Rights Act of 1964. From the outset, it had become the target for radical feminists fighting to ensure that the prescripts from Title VII were protected and enforced.

There have been several important Federal Court cases that emerged during the radical feminist era which challenged the status quo of limited opportunities for women. In March of 1969, in the case of *Weeks v. Southern Bell*, the Fifth United States Circuit Court of Appeals concluded that Lorena Weeks had been the victim of sexual discrimination under Title VII of Civil Rights Act of 1964. Weeks had been a secretary with Southern Bell in Louisiana, had been restricted from the higher-paying employment as a switchman because of a 30-pound lifting limit. Because Weeks was a woman, she was not even considered for the job.

In court, Baton Rouge attorney Sylvia Roberts for NOW argued this first sex discrimination case to come up under the provisions of Title VII. In what is considered the pivotal moment of the case, Roberts instructed Weeks to carry her typewriter—which weighed more than 30 pounds—into the courtroom.

In his opinion, Judge Johnson wrote:

> Southern Bell has clearly not met the burden here. They introduced no evidence concerning the lifting abilities of women. Rather, they would have us "assume" on the basis of "stereotyped characterization"

that few or no women can safely lift 30 pounds, while all men are treated as if they can. While one might accept, arguendo, that men are stronger on average than women, it is not clear that any conclusions about relative lifting ability would follow. This is because it can be argued tenably that technique is as important as strength in determining lifting ability. Technique is hardly a function of sex. What does seem clear is that using these class stereotypes denies desirable positions to a great many women perfectly capable of performing the duties involved (United States Court of Appeals, 5th Circuit, 1969).

Another important case was decided on November 22, 1971, by the United States Supreme Court in the case of *Reed v Reed*. Sally Reed of Idaho had sued her separated husband Cecil over the right to administer the estate of their late son, which was less than $1,000. It was the first decision by Supreme Court which ruled a law that discriminated on the basis of sex was a violation of the Equal Protection Clause of 14th amendment. In a unanimous decision, the Supreme Court decided that it was unconstitutional for the state of Idaho to arbitrarily give a man preference as estate executor over a woman simply due to administrative convenience.

Justice Warren Berger writes the opinion of the court:

> To give mandatory preference to members of either sex over members of the other, merely to accomplish the elimination of hearings on the merits, is to make the very kind of arbitrary legislative choice forbidden by the Equal Protection Clause of the Fourteenth Amendment (Stetson 1997, 34).

The case was argued by ACLU lawyer Ruth Bader Ginsburg who, in 1993, would be the second woman named to the United States Supreme Court.

Works Cited

Berkeley, Kathleen, C., *The Women's Liberration Movement in America*, Westport, CT: Greenwood Press, 1999, 28, 60, 105.

Bromberg, Sarah, *Feminist Issues in Prostitution*, paper presented at International Conference on Prostitution, Cal State University, Northridge, 1997, 6–7.

Brownmiller, Susan, *Against Our Will: Men, Women, and Rape*, www.susanbrown miller.com/susanbrownmiller/html/against_our_will.html.

Brownmiller, Susan, "Speaking Out on Prostitution", Koedt, Ann, ed., *Radical Feminism*, New York: Quadrangle Books, 76.

Echols, Alice, *Daring to Be Bad, Radical Feminism in America, 1967–1975*, Minneapolis: University of Minnesota Press, 1989, viii, xiv, 6.

Freeman, Jo, "The Building of the Gilded Cage," *Notes from the Third Year*, New York Radical Women, 1971, 139.

Griswold v. Connecticut, Justice William O. Douglas, Opinion of the Court, Supreme Court of the United States, June 7, 1965, Cornell University Law School, www.law.cornell.edu/supct/html/historic.USSC_CR_0381_0479.ZO.html.

Guttmacher Institute, "Alan F. Guttmacher, 1898–1974," 2008, (www.guttmacher .org/about/alan-bio.html).

Hull, N. E. H. and Hoffer, Peter Charles, *Roe v. Wade: The Abortion Rights Controversy in American History*, Witchita: University of Kansas Press, 2001, 201.

Kohn, George C., *Dictionary of Historical Documents*, New York, Facts on File, 1991, 143.

Priesand, Rabbi Sally, *Judaism and the New Woman*, New York: W.W. Norton & Company, 1996, xiii–xiv.

O'Beirne, Kate, *Women Who Make the World Worse and How Their Radical Feminist Assault Is Ruining Our Family, Military, School, and Sports*, New York: Sentinel, 2006, 48.

Solanas, Valerie, *SCUM Manifesto*, 1967.

Stetson, Dorothy McBride, *Women's Rights in the USA, Policy Debates and Gender Roles*, New York: Garland Publishing, Inc., 1997, 34.

Tax, Meredith, "Woman and Her Mind: The Story of Everyday Life," *Notes from the Second Year*, 1969, 4.

United States Court of Appeals for the Fifth Circuit, March 4, 1969, 7 (408 F.2d228; U.S.App.Lexis 13419; 70 L.R.R.M. 2843; 1 Fair Empl. Prac.).

Willis, Ellen, "Forward," Echols, Alice, *Daring to Be Bad, Radical Feminism in America, 1967–1975*, Minneapolis: University of Minnesota Press, 1989, ix.

Legislation and Legacy

The Equal Rights Amendment

Throughout the 1970s some of the movement's efforts began to manifest themselves in the form of federal legislation. The year 1972 initiated the drive to pass one of the most controversial constitutional amendments in history. Reflecting the influence that radical feminism and the women's movement began to exert on American Society, on March 22, the United States Senate passed the Equal Rights Amendment (ERA) by a vote of 84 to 8, clearing the way for ratification by the states. The ERA had already passed the House of Representatives in the spring of 1971, and now needed ratification by 38 of the 50 states to become a permanent addition to the Constitution.

The text of the Amendment read:

1. Equality of rights under law shall not be denied or abridged by the United States or by any State on account of sex.
2. The Congress shall have the power to enforce, by appropriate legislation, the provisions of this article.

3. This amendment shall take effect two years after the date of ratification.

The Equal Rights Amendment was originally presented in 1923, under Alice Paul's National Women's Party, but passage remained stalled for 49 years. Proponents of the ERA felt the issue of women's rights needed to be cemented into the Constitution for their ideal to become a reality. Opponents claimed that ERA would deny a woman's right to be supported by her husband, and privacy rights would be overturned. Fears of the ERA would help create a powerful conservative backlash, ushering in a new conservative era in the 1980s.

Roe v. Wade

On January 22, 1973, the United States Supreme Court ruled in a 7–2 decision in the case of *Roe v Wade*, that states may not restrict a woman's right to abortion during the first trimester of pregnancy. It further ruled that during the second trimester, the state may limit the right only to safeguard woman's health:

> The case involved pseudonym Jane Roe, an impoverished Texas woman who wanted to end the pregnancy caused by a rape. The Supreme Court declares the Texas anti-abortion statute unconstitutional, a violation to a woman's right to personal privacy. The Court stated the fetus was not a person within the meaning of the Fourteenth Amendment, and the state had no "compelling interest" in protecting prenatal life until viable. (Kohn, 1991, 283–284)

However, the Court bypassed the question of when life begins, which has clouded the debate over abortion ever since.

In 1967, prior to *Roe v. Wade*, 49 states still considered abortion a felony, and 42 states permitted abortions only in cases of threat to the mother's life. The procedure carried a tremendous stigma which made even discussion impermissible. Reformers and doctors regaled horror stories of botched "back-alley" abortions performed by untrained practitioners or, worse, the desperate women themselves. But since the

1965 landmark case *Griswold v. Connecticut*—which legitimized the disbursement of contraceptive information to married couples—reformers emphasized the decision to get an abortion as inherent under the right to privacy alluded to under the 14th Amendment. Reformers also declared that the primary issue is not the abortion procedure, but that a woman—under her right to privacy—had the ultimate right to decide whether to subject her body and her life to the effects, perils, and costs of giving birth.

The Supreme Court's decision would polarize the nation between those who believe the government should step in to protect the lives of the unborn, and those who believe the course of the prenatal experience should be left up to the individual mother. It would raise questions such as whether sentient life begins at conception, at birth, or somewhere in between. Arguments about abortion would pit the life and health of the unborn with that of the mother. And it would press for the decision about who has ultimate control of a woman's body: the government, or the individual woman.

In 1976, the Supreme Court would strike down the Missouri state requirement of parental consent for women to obtain abortions. The Court would continue to rule that prohibiting contraceptives for persons under 17 is unconstitutional.

The Conservative Backlash

The decision in *Roe v. Wade*—along with the passage of the ERA—seemed to help energize the conservative right, creating a backlash against the progress of the women's liberation movement. Particularly damaging to the ERA were the efforts of conservative attorney Phyllis Schafly, who mobilized her "Stop the ERA" movement. Schafly and her supporters feared the passage of the ERA would remove privileges of the American woman, including "dependent wife" benefits under Social Security and exemption from the military draft.

By the time Schafly started her campaign in 1972, the drive for ratification seemed to be surging forward successfully, with Hawaii having become the first state to ratify on the very day the amendment passed the Senate. By early 1973, 24 states had ratified the 50-year-old amendment. However, due largely to the efforts of Schafly and her supporters, the drive stalled considerably until 1977, when Indiana became the 34th and last state to ratify.

According to the Congressional statute, the states had seven years from the date of Congressional passage to ratify. ERA supporters such as NOW managed to have the deadline extended from 1979 to 1982. But the ratification drive bogged down during the conservative administration of Ronald Reagan.

Historically, the ERA pitted those who wanted special treatment of women to compensate for years of discrimination versus those who wanted complete equality between men and women. But radical feminists saw the ERA as an attempt to co-opt women into the dysfunctional oppressive system. They rejected the ERA as reform within a hopelessly broken system. In any case, the failure of the ratification of the ERA may have tolled the death knell for the radical feminist era.

Under the general label of "Family Values," the conservative point of view discounted the importance of child care, equal opportunity in work, sexual orientation, and access to contraception or abortion. The New Right drummed up fears that the effect of the feminist movement would dilute those values. They suggested that radical feminists came from dysfunctional families, and their points of view represented a skewed minority. They claimed that wage disparities are not due to "sex discrimination but rather the result of choices mothers freely make in their desire to work and balance family responsibility" (O'Beirne 2006, 48). Conservatives also asserted that violence against women was severely exaggerated by feminists, and "domestic violence is most common in the transitory, free-form co-habitational relationships that feminists have long celebrated as replacements for traditional marriage" (Fagan et al. 1995, 7). They claimed that women should not be put in harm's way in the military, but should be home taking care of the children, and leaving the fighting to the men. They asserted that feminists minimized the needs of children and families over the selfish pursuits of adults, such as promiscuity and homosexuality.

The conservatives insisted that the "erosion of marriage is also principal factor behind growth of welfare state" (Fagan et al. 1995, 7) and that "foremost is the positive impact of marriage in alleviating poverty among mothers and children" (Fagan et al. 1995, 6). They maintained there are inherent differences in men and women that create natural gender roles, but that differences did not mean inequality. They asserted that feminist-supported increases in educational, athletic, and economic opportunities for women merely decreased opportunities for men, who are the natural breadwinners.

But the radical feminists asserted that for the New Right, what men "can" do is valued more than what women "can" do, and fighting is valued more than birthing. Actually, said the radical feminists, these tasks should not be labeled "male or female" but due to individual differences. Difficulties arise—among feminists and antifeminists—when one individual trait is assumed for all men or all women.

This conservative backlash helped to derail the ratification of the ERA by 1977, as the New Right preached its horror about the effects of *Roe v. Wade* and the ERA on "Family Values." The Right admonished the *Roe v. Wade* decision, which they said legalized murder, undermined traditional family roles, and allowed women to be as promiscuous as men. The conservative response ushered in the passage of the Hyde Amendment in 1977, which nullified federal funding for abortions for poor women.

Legacy

The 2008 Presidential Campaign was a great illustration of the lasting effects of the radical feminism. For the Democrats, Hillary Clinton became the first women presidential candidate recognized, from the outset, as the favorite to win. On the GOP side, Sarah Palin, became the first Republican woman candidate for vice-president. Although many questioned Palin's qualifications for the second highest office in the land, nobody seemed to use Palin's gender as a viable reason. Although both women lost their campaigns, the reasons they lost had nothing to do with being women; it had to do with their qualifications in the eyes of the voters. The idea of a woman in the Oval Office had become an acceptable proposal.

The effect of the radical feminist era was essentially to raise the stakes in American society's contract for the rights and opportunities for women. Because much of the radical feminists' vision seemed so extreme to much of America, their actions opened minds to the possibilities of some of their goals. Comparatively, more opportunity for women in the workplace and in education, and more autonomous control over themselves and their bodies seemed not only possible but justified. Once again in American history, the role of the radical element—such as the radical feminists in the women's liberation movement—seems to be to push the liberal element towards areas of reform that it otherwise would not have explored. There always has to be someone in the crowd willing to say "the emperor has no clothes."

It is true that the radical feminists were not able to change the social order of America the way they wanted. The fate of all radical movements in this country has been that enough of the citizens of the United States have been satisfied with the country to resist any drastic replacement of the current system. Such is, as Clecak puts it, the "massive power and essential stability of American Social order" (Clecak 1973, 15). As opportunity for women increased, the need for radical feminism decreased. Fewer women saw the need to overthrow the prevailing American way of life but supported reformations in policy and custom that support increased power and opportunity for women.

What ended the radical feminist era also brought the ideals and goals of feminism to a larger and more receptive audience. More middle-of-the-road organizations such as NOW brought the ideas fermented in radical feminism to a liberal audience open to new ideas. Although this audience was open to reform ideas that brought more opportunity and equality to women, most of America could not accept the radical notion of revolution, which would tear down the current societal culture to replace it with a new one. As the reformative ideas of the radical feminists reached a broader audience, the impetus behind the radical feminist revolution was replaced with changes in the policies and practices of American culture, providing women with more power and opportunity. The "personal is political" of Carol Hanisch—which originally meant to emphasize the need for political action—ended up emphasizing the need for personal insight and change. It asserts that freedom begins with the individual, because individual freedom begets social freedom.

The era of the radical feminists featured several rifts among segments of the movement, which kept them from uniting into a more successful political force. One rift separated those who emphasized political action over consciousness-raising as the key to change in the individual, and subsequently change in society. There was also a gap between those feminists who blamed all men for the oppression of women, and those who blamed the capitalistic, patriarchal system, at the root of the oppression of women *and* men. There was a rift between those from the upper class, and those from the working class, who often felt unrecognized by the radical feminists. There were also rifts between white women and women of color, who appeared to be largely unrepresented among the radical feminists, and further gulfs existed between lesbians and those who did not want them represented in the movement.

All of these divergences served to dilute the power and focus of the radical feminists. And as the energy behind radical feminism dissipated, it opened the door for liberal, reform-minded feminism to settle into the minds of mainstream America. The finger pointing and name-calling among the feminists damaged the cohesion of the radical feminism, which often failed to recognize the differences in women. Early radical feminism valued a fantasy notion of gender unity, overlooking class and race differences and thus failing to acknowledge and include them. Additionally, liberal feminism entities avoided the male-domination bent in order to avoid the alienation of men, and of women in relationship with men. Liberal feminism linked oppression to the economic system at large, which victimized men as well as women. Liberal feminism focused its concern on liberation of the individual over remaking society. In the end, radicalism fed off dissent, while liberalism was built on inclusion.

As liberal feminism recognized the differences in women, it became more inclusive, less radical, and more prominent. NOW and *MS.* magazine—along with its spokesperson and figurehead Gloria Steinham—attracted a larger, more diverse following than the radical feminists could ever muster. Many radical feminists saw Steinham as a relative newcomer with little credibility, and resented Steinham's media coronation as spokesperson for women's movement. In 1975 the Redstockings accused Steinham and *MS.* of being a CIA front, which worked to disperse the radical feminist movement. *MS.* and Steinham were seen as colluding with the very system that many radical feminists originally sought to overturn. To be a viable

commercial system, *MS.* had to play within the capitalistic system—
something that many of the early radical feminists found abhorrent.
Its advertisements were seen as commercialism targeted for the feminist. Many radical feminist writers resented *MS.* for using writers from
the outside, and not tapping the knowledge and ability which founded
the movement in the first place. Ellen Willis resigned from *MS.* in
June of 1975, citing differences with the magazine's conservative, capitalistic brand of feminism. But alas, this liberal, middle-of-the-road
feminism was able to gather the resources and capabilities to reach a
mainstream audience, thus assuring its stability beyond the end of
the radical feminist era.

The degree of success achieved by the radical feminists depends
largely on one's point of view. From a revolutionary viewpoint, the
movement did nothing to overturn the oppressive economic and
class-based society, from which all the social ills—including discrimination and exploitation of women—are thought to stem.

But despite the eventual dissolution of radical feminism, its impact
can be recognized, particularly in the realm of higher education. Many
of the radical feminists profiled in this text went on to find positions in
colleges and universities, generally in the area of women's studies:
Ti-Grace Atkinson at Tufts University; Rosalyn Baxandall at SUNY,
Old Westbury; Charlotte Bunch at Rutgers University; Mary Daly at
Boston College; Dana Densmore at St. John's College; Roxanne Dunbar at California State University, Hayward; Jo Freeman at SUNY;
Barbara Winslow at Brooklyn College; and Naomi Weisstein at
SUNY Buffalo. Others—such as Rita Mae Brown, Susan Brownmil-
ler, Kate Millett, Shulamith Firestone, Robin Morgan—exerted their
influence as writers through the media.

> Radical feminism had a major influence, for example, on the
> intellectual formation of faculty who would go on to develop
> women's studies, which, in turn, had a major impact on main-
> streaming core principles of second-wave feminism within the
> nation's colleges and universities. Radical feminism also spawned,
> for instance, the anti-rape and anti-domestic violence movements,
> touching the lives of countless women through hotlines, shelters,
> and community supports. Betty Friedan's *McCall's* columns, side
> by side with *MS.* magazine, played a crucial role in making the

women's movement attractive to women in America's heartland. Without the contribution of either of these forces, feminism and its philosophies would have failed to achieve the far-reaching influence across American culture that it did, so fast, and so early on (Siegel 2007, 169).

Alice Echols, in her book *Daring to Be Bad* (1989), reflects on the effects of the radical feminist age:

> If radical feminism failed to survive as a movement, its effects were hardly evanescent. Although women's situation in the late 1980s falls far short of the radical vision, the world today is nonetheless vastly different than what it was twenty years ago. While one can point to other factors—technological advances in birth control, the expansion of the tertiary factor, the "male revolt" against the breadwinner ethic, and the collapse of the family wage system, which in term has made dual-income families a necessity—radical feminism was central to this transformation. By challenging the phallocentrism of normative sexuality, radical feminists have contributed to the restructuring of heterosexual sex. As a result of radical feminism's affirmation of female desire, women today are more apt to assert their sexual needs. Both the legalization of abortion and the public awareness of rape (reflected in revised rape laws) have done a great deal to further women's sexual self-determination. By exposing the sexism of the medical profession, questioning the omniscience of the physician, and promoting self-help techniques, radical feminists have encouraged women to take a more active role in their health care. Radical feminism's assault on the nuclear family and institutionalized heterosexuality have made it possible (if not easy) for people to fashion alternatives to nuclear family and heterosexuality. And while housework and child care remain far too much women's work, there has been an erosion of the sexual division of labor in the home—as a consequence both of changed economic conditions and of radical feminism. Finally, although gender is far from meaningless in our culture, our cultural definitions of masculinity and femininity are today far less rigid and constraining than was the case before the resurgence of feminist activism in the late 60s (Echols 1989, 285).

Even the use of the pronoun "Ms." would not have come into common usage without the influence of radical feminist thought over the women's movement.

What the radical feminists did more than anything is emphatically highlight the oppressions with which all women—to some degree—can identify, and with which enlightened men can empathize. And their advocacy led to greater opportunities for women within the larger system which, apparently, most Americans do not want to eliminate.

Writers like Elizabeth Fox-Genoee and Katie Roiphe describe how today's empowered women are often no longer empathetic with message of older feminists. They see the older feminists blaming others for their discontent, creating a cult of victimization. To the average woman trying to get ahead in her well-established career, the women's movement can seems irrelevant. To those who enjoy their femininity and power at the same time, the feminists can seem sexually protective and humorless.

Yet the effect of the radical feminists did not seem to completely escape the later generation. In 1992, a CNN/Time Poll showed that 77 percent felt the women's movement made life better, 94 percent felt the women's movement made women more independent, and 82 percent saw how the movement improved women's lives. Yet only 33 percent of the same sample would identify herself as feminist. It seems today's empowered women may no longer be empathetic with message of older feminists—the one's that made the power possible in the first place (Siegel 2007, 115).

Writer Ellen Willis reminisces on the kind of world that existed before the influence of the radical feminists:

> I remember a kind of blatant, taken for granted, un-self-conscious sexism that no one could get away with today pervading every aspect of life. I remember . . . wanting to take a course at Columbia and being told to my face that the professor didn't want "girls" in his class because they weren't serious enough. I remember, as a young journalist, being asked by an editor to use only my first initials in my byline because the magazine had too many women writers. I remember having to wear uncomfortable clothes, girdles, and stiff bras and high heels. I remember being afraid to have sex because I might get pregnant, and too intense to enjoy it because I might get

pregnant. I remember the panic of a late period. I remember when a friend of a friend came to New York for an illegal abortion, remember us trying to decide whether her pain and fever were bad enough to warrant going to the hospital and then worrying that we had waited too long, remember her fear of admitting what was wrong, and her doctor yelling at her for "going to a quack" and refusing to reassure her that she would live. I remember I was supposed to feel flattered when men hassled me on the street, and be polite and tactful when my dates wouldn't take no for an answer, and have a "good reason" for refusing. I remember, too, feeling pleased to be different from other women—better—because I was ambitious and contemptuous of domesticity and "thought like a man," while at the same time, in my personal and sexual relationships with men, I was constantly reminded that I was, after all, "only a woman." I remember the peculiar alienation that comes of having one's self-respect be contingent on "self-hatred" (Echols, 1989, 115).

Davidson, in *Oppressed Majority*, continued the retrospective:

These experiences unnerved me, despite reminders that I should not take it personally and understanding of what lay behind the fear and hostility. The negative reactions toward me expressed a great deal of what women's liberation is about: women's long-suppressed anger at being used; women's sense of vulnerability and defenselessness; women's suspicion and mistrust of other women; women's insecurity, lack of confidence in their judgments; "the secret fear" as one girl put it, "that maybe we are inferior" (Davidson 1969, 4).

Ultimately, the result of the feminist movement—spearheaded by the radical feminists—was one of choice. Not just the freedom of choice between alternatives, as Mills would put it, but the opportunity to select the alternatives from which to choose. This includes a woman's choice of what to do with her body; to choose who she loves; whether or not to have children; and what profession she chooses. Measures for women don't necessarily mean that all women have to do this, but they all should have the opportunity; not all women want what feminists want, but all should have the opportunities to choose. The legacy of the radical feminists is choice; not only freedom of choice, but access to alternatives among which to choose. The radical feminist expanded the alternatives for not only women, but men, gays, people of color, people with disabilities, and so forth.

Finally, Rosalyn Baxandall places the radical feminist era in personal perspective:

> The one thing that I do have against the books that are written, is they talk about all the politics and the splits, et cetera, but they don't talk about all the joy and fun we had. It was wonderful being there . . . It was the most joy I've known in my life. It was wonderful. We knew we were changing history, and it was terrific (Ceballos 1991, 62).

Works Cited

Ceballos, Jacqueline Michot, *Interview with Rosalyn Fraad Baxandall*, Cambridge: The Radcliffe Institute for Advanced Study, 1991, 62.

Clecak, Peter, *Radical Paradoxes*, New York: Harper & Row Publishers, 1968, 15.

Davidson, Sara, "An Oppressed Majority Demands Its Rights," *Life Magazine*, 1969, 4.

Echols, Alice, *Daring to Be Bad, Radical Feminism in America*, 1967–1975, Minneapolis: University of Minnesota Press, 1989, 115, 285.

Fagan, Patrick, Rector, Robert E., and Noyes, Loren R., *Why Congress Should Ignore Radical Feminists' Opposition to Marriage*, The Heritage Foundation, 1995–2004, 6–7.

Kohn, George C., *Dictionary of Historical Documents*, New York, Facts on File, 1991, 283–285.

O'Beirne, Kate, *Women Who Make the World Worse and How Their Radical Feminist Assault Is Ruining Our Families, Military, School, and Sports*, New York: Sentinel, 2006, 16.

Siegel, Deborah, *Sisterhood Interrupted*, New York: Palgrave McMillan, 2007, 169.

Biographical Sketches

The following are profiles of some of the most prominent personalities of the radical feminist era.

Jane Alpert

Jane Alpert was a New Left fugitive turned radical feminist in 1969. She was arrested by the FBI on November 19, 1969 for conspiring with Sam Melville of the Weatherman and Pat Swinton of the North American Congress on Latin America, to bomb buildings such as Chase Manhattan, New York Federal Building, Standard Oil, New York Police Head-quarters, and the Armed Forces Induction Center. She was arrested while members of the group planted bombs in National Guard trucks. She pled guilty, then skipped bail and fled underground in May, 1970. She stayed underground for four and a half years, working low-level jobs, keeping alias names. While on the lam, she joined a women's consciousness-raising group, as she renounced what she saw as the patri-archal left, becoming a committed radical feminist.

In 1974 she mailed a manifesto called *Mother Right: A New Feminist Theory,* to *MS.* magazine. With it, Albert urged "women to leave

the left and leftist causes and begin working for women, for ourselves."
(Alpert 1974, 2). She believed in the "feminist revolution ... in which
the society-wide recognition of the creative principle as female will
take the place of worship of the modern male (God)." (Albert 1974, 3).
Mother Right would have a profound influence on the women's movement, seen as a counterpoint to the factionalism that was tearing asunder
the cause.

Of her time in the underground, Alpert wrote:

> As I moved around, I could see more clearly than ever the
> oppression of black, Chicano, Puerto Rican and Indian peoples. Yet
> at the same time I was learning concretely that women existed in
> well-defined subcultures within each white and Third World com-
> munity ... Men, Third World or otherwise, young and old, hippie
> and straight, related to me as Woman, all my other interests or char-
> acteristics being, in their eyes, mere modifications of that one essen-
> tial. Whether I was desired, rejected, abused, admired, ignored,
> treated with kindness or hostility, it was basically because I was a
> female doing whatever I was doing.
>
> I could see women everywhere—white, black, brown, Indian—
> responding in their daily lives to the fact that some women some-
> where had said, "Men oppress us." I came to know Chicano women
> living in a barrio who were organizing, women's health-care pro-
> grams and women's anti-rape squadrons to patrol their own neigh-
> borhood ... they demonstrated to me, among others, that the
> changing consciousness represented by the Women's Movement has
> been far more far-reaching than any public-opinion poll on Women's
> Liberation would seem to show (Alpert 1974, 6).

In *Mother Right*, Alpert proclaimed the essential but unrecognized
and undervalued role of mothers in society. Albert saw mothers as the
vanguard of the revolutionary class, that group which is not only
greatly exploited by the class in power, but which is also performing
labor which is essential to the functioning of society:

> ... for there is very clearly a large group of women who by reason
> of both exploitation and importance to society perfectly answer the
> requirements of the vanguard, and who are increasingly closely in

touch with one another. These women are, of course, mothers. The labor of these women in the home . . . cannot be replaced on a mass scale without cataclysmic changes in the social structure (Alpert 1974, 11).

She also pronounced the power of the inherent mother in each woman as ideal force by which to revolutionize society. For Alpert, matriarchy meant nothing less than the end of oppression. The point of the *Mother Right* is to reshape the family according to the perceptions of women, and to reshape society in the image of the new matriarchal family.

It is conceivable that the intrinsic biological connection between mother and embryo or mother and infant gives rise to the psychological qualities which have always been linked with women, both in ancient lore and modern behavioral science.

The qualities coming to the fore are the same ones a mother projects in the best kind of nurturing relationship, to a child: empathy, intuitiveness, adaptability, awareness of growth as a process rather than as goal-ended, inventiveness, protective feelings toward others, and the capacity to respond emotionally as well as rationally.

Many segments of the Women's Movement are now beginning to explicitly recognize this truth and to act upon it. NOW is making a major push to speak to the needs of housewives by agitating for an end to discrimination against married women by banks, insurance companies, and credit union . . . The uprising of women . . . must be an affirmation of the power of female consciousness, of the Mother (Alpert 1974,12).

Jane Alpert surrendered to authorities November 4, 1974, and was sentenced to 27 months in prison. She was sentenced to another 4 months for contempt of court, for refusing to testify at 1975 trial of another defendant. However, some accused Alpert of informing against other fugitives. Many thought Alpert had squealed when Swinton was arrested on March 12, 1975. But Alpert refused to testify, and Swinton was eventually acquitted.

Jane Alpert was born on May 20, 1947, and grew up in New York City. Her grandfather Abraham Kahane was a socialist, and her grandparents were Russian Jews. Her mother graduated from high school at 14, from Hunter College at 18. Her brother Skip was blind, suffering respiratory difficulties which permanently stunted his growth. His need reportedly took most if not all of Jane's mother's attention. Jane and her family moved to Uniontown, Pennsylvania, where she felt like an outsider because she was Jewish and from the city. She reportedly had the attention of her father when young, because mother concentrated on Skip. Her father paid less attention to her, however, as his business failed and he suffered a nervous breakdown.

Alpert attended Forest Hills High School, 1960, where she was introduced to the works of Ayn Rand. She also attended Swarthmore College, majoring in classic literature and graduating with honors in 1967. She did some graduate work at Columbia University, and got a job as an editorial assistant with Cambridge University Press.

Delving into the New Left, Alpert wrote for the underground newspaper *RAT*, and became involved in the Black Panther movement. She met Sam Melville at the Community Action Coalition. The two became involved romantically, and moved in together. The combination of sexual love and radical ideology seemed to become more than Alpert could resist. Later, of her lover and fellow fugitive, she would write, "Yet I have seen his behavior duplicated in the most bourgeois households by males of political persuasions, economic backgrounds, ages, and skin colors." Melville eventually died in the Attica Prison riots in 1971

Jane Alpert would go on to write *Growing Up Underground (1981)* a personal, provocative account of her life on the run between 1970 and 1974.

For *Mother Right*, Alpert would further write:

> As patriarchal reasoning went, since "God" or "Nature" or "evolution" had made women the bearer and nurse of the species, it logically followed that she should stay home with the children and perform as a matter of more-or-less ordained duty all the domestic chores involved in keeping and feeding the household. When women work outside the home, we have the most menial and lowest-paid tasks to perform, chiefly because any labor a woman performs outside the home is thought to be temporary and inessential to her.

... it contradicts our felt experience of the biological difference between the sexes as one of immense significance. Women's movement has encouraged thousands of women who would never have done so before to discover and develop their unique talents, and to stand up against male prerogatives and values with originality and courage (Alpert 1974, 8).

Ti-Grace Atkinson

Considered by many as the most radical of all radical feminists, Ti-Grace Atkinson was a militant feminist philosopher who exerted tremendous influence over—while also becoming clearly frustrated with—the feminist movement of the 60s and 70s. In her brief meteoric period with the women's movement feminists, she made abortion a key issue, and politicized sex. Atkinson viewed women as a political class oppressed by men, the enemy, and proclaimed married women as hostages.

Ti-Grace Atkinson came from a prominent, upper-class Cajun Republican family in Louisiana. She was born November 9, 1938, in Baton Rouge, Louisiana. Her name—Ti-Grace—is Cajun for "little or petite," a description that never seemed to fit this tall, highly outspoken woman. She married her high school boyfriend in 1961 at the age of 17, but divorced him six years later. She graduated from the University of Pennsylvania in 1964, with a bachelor's degree of fine arts.

At age 28 with no prior political experience, Atkinson joined NOW in 1967, a relationship that would turn out to be both fruitful and turbulent. She quickly became the president of the New York chapter of NOW, which at the time contained 30 percent of total NOW membership. However, she left NOW in 1968 because she felt the organization was too hierarchical, and did not allow enough democratic participation. She wanted to change the by-laws and powers structure of NOW, declaring that one cannot overcome a system (oppressive, patriarchal, hierarchical) that one is willing to imitate.

After leaving NOW in 1968, she initiated the October 17th Movement, founding The Feminists in October 1969. She left The Feminists in 1970, after the group passed a resolution barring members (largely Atkinson) from talking to the press.

In 1969, she visited Valerie Solanas, who was in jail for shooting Andy Warhol. Atkinson joined San Francisco's Daughters of Bilitis—the oldest lesbian organization in the country—but resigned in January of 1971.

Atkinson became known for outrageous and provocative statements. At the dedication of first Lesbian Center in America in New York City—in her speech "Strategy and Tactics: A Presentation of Political Lesbianism"—Atkinson declared that "the movement itself, so far, has neither demonstrated itself as political or organized itself to effective major change." Atkinson called feminists phonies, and regarded married women as hostages. She accused women who had sex with men as collaborators, and described lesbianism as a buffer between men and women, both sexually and politically. "Sex is overrated," she said. "If someday I have to choose between sex and freedom, there's no question I'd take freedom" (Davidson 1969, 2).

Atkinson published a collection of her thoughts and ideas called *Amazon Odyssey* (1974). She became a professor of philosophy at Tufts University in Medford, Massachusetts.

Rosalyn Baxandall

Rosalyn Baxandall represented an often unrecognized contingency within the radical feminist ranks, those who were both wives and mothers while advocating for women's liberation. As such, she supported issues which were pertinent both to the rights of women, and for the preservation of the family. In addition to being active in the New York Radical Women and Redstockings, she campaigned for welfare rights, and she was instrumental in establishing city-financed child-care facilities in New York City.

Rosalyn Fraad was born on June 12, 1939 on 95th Street in New York City. Her mother Irma London and her father Lewis Martin Fraad were lawyers, and her father was a labor organizer, and later a pediatrician. Rosalyn sprung from a long line of advocates, as Irma's mother and father were also lawyers. In fact Rosalyn's grand uncle— Meyer London—served was one of only two members of the Socialist Party of America to be elected to Congress. Rosalyn's grandmother marched in suffrage parades. Rosalyn grew up with two sisters, Harriet and Julie. When Rosalyn had an abortion later in life, she was surprised and relieved to hear her grandmother admit she had six.

Rosalyn attended PS 9 in Manhattan, and attended the all-girl Hunter High School. She read Beauvoir's *The Second Sex* when she was young, picking it up because she thought it was about sex. As it did for many of the radical feminists, *The Second Sex* seemed to set a tone for Roslyn's life to come.

Rosalyn became interested in the civil rights movement in high school, picketing Woolworth's during the sit-ins. She also joined the antiwar movement, and became a member of the SDS. In 1963, she married Lee Baxandall, writer and playwright, from Oshkosh, Wisconsin, (she would divorce him in 1983). She earned her history and French degrees at University of Wisconsin the same year, and studied sociology on a graduate level at Columbia University but did not immediately finish her graduate degree. She would eventually join the faculty at SUNY, Old Westbury, becoming the chair and a Distinguished Teaching Professor of the American Studies Department.

She went to work for Mobilization for Youth on lower East Side, where she fought to change welfare laws. Her son Phineas was born 1967 the same year she joined the women's movement. That year, she met Shulamith Firestone in 1967, after the Chicago SDS meeting. She participated in the Jeannette Rankin Parade in January 1968, and attended the Counter-Inaugural protest, in which Firestone was harassed by the SDS. Baxandall also demonstrated at the *Ladies' Home Journal* office.

Baxandall became involved in as many New York feminist groups as possible, including the New York Feminists, WITCH, Redstockings, and New York Radical Women. She helped start a child care center called "Women with Children," which took over the building on 6th street between A and B. It was eventually called "Liberation Nursery" and still exists today. She worked to change child care laws in New York, when it was illegal to have a child under two in daycare.

Baxandall was there for the 1968 Bridal Fair protest, and for the Wall Street WITCH demonstration. She also helped Betty Friedan organize the Congress to Unite Women in 1969. She also participated in the Abortion Speak Out at Washington Square. But perhaps her most interesting contribution was the scintillating interview in 1968 on *The David Susskind Show* with Kate Millett, Anselma Del'Olio, and Jacqui Ceballos.

Baxandall became a strident proponent for consciousness-raising, saying she felt it helped women understand how unequal their situations were. She admitted that she and others were not open to the lesbian contingent, and other diverse factions of women, saying:

> So we weren't sensitive enough to the fact that there are different kinds . . . that some women loved women, and we should have been more sensitive. So I don't think the lesbians divided anything. Unfortunately, that's the way it ended—this big division . . . There were splits between women who had children, too. There were splits between white women and black women. There were all kinds of splits (Ceballos 1991, 44).

But most of all, Baxandall attested to the marvelous adventure the radical feminist era had been for many women:

> The one thing that I do have against the books that are written, is they talk about all the politics and the splits, et cetera, but they don't talk about all the joy and fun we had. It was wonderful being there . . . It was the most joy I've known in my life. It was wonderful. We knew we were changing history, and it was terrific (Ceballos 1991, 63).

Heather Tobis Booth

Heather Tobis Booth has been a community organizer for more than 40 years. Her immense skills and commitment contributed heavily to the movements of the 60s, starting with the civil rights, student, and women's movement in Chicago. In 1965, she founded the organization Jane, which facilitated more than 10,000 abortions in the Chicago area. PBS aired a documentary on the organization in 1998 called JANE: An Abortion Service. Booth said about the abortions: "It wasn't that we were for abortion, we were for women having the right to make this most personal decision" (Ter 1999, 2).

Heather Tobis was born on December 15, 1945, in Brookhaven, Mississippi. Her parents, physician Jerome Sanford Tobis and Hazel Victoria Weisbard Tobis, moved the family to Bensenhurst, New

York, and eventually to Long Island. She speaks of her parents in loving tones. Although her parents were not activists, they provided a warm and loving environment which motivated their children to respond to the social problems around them. Her two brothers—David and Jonathan—grew up to be a child welfare worker and a physician, respectively.

When Heather was around the age of 10, she listened on the radio to the horrible story of Emmett Till, the 14-year-old African American who was lynched in Mississippi for reportedly whistling at a white woman.Like many other people of the time, she was inspired to action by the story. She also said she was stirred by the work of Ella Baker, the civil rights and human rights activist from Virginia. Tobis soon joined CORE in New York City, actively working against the death penalty.

Heather Tobis came to the University of Chicago in 1963, soon becoming head of the local chapter of the SNCC. She also served as the liaison between the Coordinating Council of Community organizations and helped to organize freedom schools during a citywide school boycott for quality integrated schools. In 1964, she went to Mississippi as part of Summer Project, doing Freedom School, voter registration, and MFDP freedom registration.

She also joined the SDS, Chicago. She met her future husband, Paul Booth, at a sit-in against the Vietnam War at the University of Chicago in 1966 when he was national secretary at SDS. He is now an assistant to AFSCME president Gerald McEntee.

The name Jane was selected for the abortion service to symbolize the anonymity under which the organization operated. "The Service"—as the organization was called—was initiated in 1965 when Booth searched for and found a doctor who would perform an abortion for a friend's sister. Other women began approaching Booth, and soon word spread throughout the community. Booth organized a staff, and Jane began providing the much needed service for women through the Chicago area and beyond. Abortion at the time was still illegal, and women who found themselves with an unwanted pregnancy had few options available to them. The Jane staff took the time to be warm and supportive to the often frightened women; they would arrange for a doctor to perform the abortion or—for those who could not afford the sliding-scale fee—they would instruct the woman how to perform safe abortions on themselves. By 1970, more than one hundred women had worked for Jane, which facilitated as many as one hundred abortions per week.

After reading the Mary King-Casey Hayden document *Sex and Caste: A Kind of Memo* in 1966, Booth helped initiate the first campus women's movement, called the Women's Radical Action Program. She was also instrumental in launching the Westside Group, originally a politico group which became a core gathering for women's liberation, launching both action and consciousness-raising activities. At the August 1967 SDS National Conference on New Politics in Chicago, the women's agenda was virtually ignored by the New Left men. One week later she attended a meeting to organize the first autonomous women's liberation group, the Chicago Women's Liberation Union. The CWLU offered both work and discussion groups, and launched the nation's first women's movement newsletter, *The Voice for Women's Liberation.* Booth, Vivian Rothstein, Amy Kesselman, and Naomi Weisstein became the *Gang of Four* described by Kesselman in *The Feminist Memoirs Project.* Other members included Sara Evans Boyte (*Personal Politics*, 1979), Ellen Dubois, and Sue Munaker.

Booth's career as a community organizer continued long after her participation in the CWLU. She became a teacher for high school dropouts, where she was denied a job when she took maternity leave. She directed the Action Committee for Decent Childcare (ACDC), helping to win an unprecedented $1 million for city funded childcare. In 1973, she won a back pay suit for the National Labor Relations Board, and used the money to found Midwest Academy in Chicago, a training center for social organizers, which helped prepare workers and develop strategic plans for Sierra Club, NARAL, United States Student Organization, and many others. In 2000 she became the executive director of the National Association for the Advancement of Colored People's (NAACP) National Voter Fund. She has provided international consulting with prodemocracy organizations, and has consulted with groups such as MoveOn.org, Campaign for America's Future, NOW, and many others.

She has worked in numerous political campaigns, first in Chicago. She was deputy field director for Mayor Harold Washington and training director for the Democratic National Committee from 1995–1998. She also ran the outreach for the Clinton health care campaign. She was the initial consultant in the creation of the Campaign for Comprehensive Immigration Reform, and directed the health care campaign for the AFL-CIO in 2008. She led the campaign to pass President Barack Obama's first budget in 2009, and is now (2010) director of Americans for Financial Reform, to regulate the financial industry.

Heather Tobis Booth lives with her husband Paul in Washington, DC, and has two children and three grandchildren. She says it is important to remember what life was like for women before the radical feminist era. She reminds people that if we organize, we can change the world.

Rita Mae Brown

Rita Mae Brown became one of the earliest and most fiery advocates for gay issues and rights within the radical feminist movement. An early editor for the New York NOW newsletter, Brown raised consciousness about lesbianism and class differences within the women's movement. She clashed with NOW President Betty Friedan over the reality of lesbianism, and continued to advocate for gay rights throughout her luminous career.

Rita Mae Brown was born on November 28, 1944, in Hanover, Pennsylvania to an unmarried teenager named Juliann Young. Placed in an orphanage in Pittsburgh, she was adopted by Ralph and Julia Ellen Brown, a cousin of her biological mother. She moved with her adoptive family to Fort Lauderdale, Florida, in 1955, where Ralph died in 1961. She grew up in a working class home with a limited income, which perhaps set as a major life theme the struggle between the haves and the have-nots.

In 1962, she enrolled in the University of Florida on a scholarship, but she struggled to fit in. She had developed a growing interest in the civil rights movement, for which she received a reprimand. But the real controversy turned out to be her sexual orientation. Within the oppressive atmosphere, she had been ordered to undergo psychiatric therapy for lesbianism, and ostracized by university community. She left the University of Florida in 1964 to enroll at Broward Junior College.

In 1968 Rita Mae moved to New York and New York University, again gaining admission on a scholarship. She received her degree in English at NYU (and would go on to earn her PhD from Institute for Policy Studies in Washington, DC.) Brown found more acceptance in New York for her lifestyle, and helped found one of the first city's gay and lesbian student organizations, the Student Homophile League. She inadvertently became caught up in the famous Stonewall Riots in June of 1969. She would later narrate a documentary on the riots called *Before Stonewall.*

A year earlier she had joined the New York chapter of NOW, becoming the newsletter editor for the largest and most radical chapter of NOW. But like everywhere else, Rita Mae Brown ran into conflict for her lifestyle, and NOW maneuvered her out of power when she came out as gay. Many within NOW felt the issue of lesbianism would ruin efforts by NOW to outreach to the women in the mainstream. Betty Friedan reportedly referred to lesbianism as "the lavender menace" and had tried to censor Brown's efforts to have NOW acknowledge lesbianism as a feminist issue. "Betty Friedan got rid of me in a hurry," Brown conceded later, but also described Friedan as a "fundamentally moral person and about 20 years later she apologized to me in public." (Sachs 3, 2008). Indeed, Brown would have the last word on the subject.

In 1970, after leaving NOW, Brown became a founding member of Radicalesbians, and helped write the position paper "The Woman-Identified Woman." Brown was the leading participant in the group's 1970 "lavender menace" demonstration at the Second Congress to Unite Women.

In 1971, Brown moved to Washington, DC to help found "The Furies" collective. The Furies saw lesbianism not just as a sexual orientation, but as a political choice. Brown was purged from the Furies in March 1972 due to conflict around the presence of children within the collective.

In 1971, long after Brown resigned from NOW, the organization concluded at a NOW conference, "the governing board recognized the futility of ignoring the 'lavender menace' by passing a resolution 'acknowledging the oppression of lesbians as a legitimate concern of feminism.' " This resolution became a huge boost to the cause of lesbian—and gay—rights in America. A year later, NOW actually established a Task Force on Sexuality and Lesbianism. Rita Mae Brown had indeed "won the war."

Rita Mae Brown is an essayist, poet, novelist, mystery writer, and screenwriter. Brown was nominated for an Emmy in 1982; she won the Writer's Guild award for the screenplay *I Love Liberty*. She is also the author of 37 books, including *The Hand That Cradles the Rock* (1971), *A Plain Brown Rapper* (1976), and *Rita Will: Memoir of a Literary Rabble Rouser (1997)*. Her most famous work, *Rubyfruit Jungle* (1973), had been rejected by numerous mainstream publishers, finally published by a small "women's only" press Daughters Publishing Company. The publisher paid her $1,000, and the book sold 70 thousand copies. Finally, Bantam Press picked it up in 1977, printing more than 500 thousand copies. As of 2008, more than 1 million copies have been sold.

Throughout the years Brown's romantic relationships have drawn the attention of the media. She maintained a three-year relationship with tennis icon Martina Navratilova. The relationship proved both curious and controversial, for it involved two women who were both well-known and successful. The love of her life turned out to be Fannie Flagg, actress and author of *Fried Green Tomatoes at the Whistle Stop Café*.

Now 54 years old, Brown lives in Charlottesville, Virginia, where she writes, advocates for animals, and still manages to issue stimulating comments on pertinent issues. For example, on the topic of gay marriage she says: "I don't understand it (gay marriage). I don't even know why straight people want to get married because you invite the government into your bedroom" (Sachs 2008, 3).

Susan Brownmiller

Susan Brownmiller is a writer and former actress who became active with New York Radical Feminists, helping to plan and implement the *Ladies' Home Journal* protest in 1970, with Media Women. She helped organize the Speak Out on Rape conference in 1971, then went on to published *Against Our Will: Men, Women, and Rape* in 1975. She also was a contributor to *Notes from the Third Year*.

Susan Brownmiller was born on the birthday of Susan B. Anthony, February 15, in the year 1935. But she confesses on her website that this coincidence did not prove as significant as it might have, particularly when she was younger: "Did this give me a mystic identification with the great champion of women's suffrage? Nope. It bothered me that she wasn't pretty" (Brownmiller, 2009).

She was born in Brooklyn, where her father Samuel Warhaftig was a sales clerk at Macy's, and her mother Mae a secretary at the Empire State Building. Susan herself worked as a file clerk and a waitress as a young woman.

She graduated from Cornell University in Ithaca, New York in 1955 and she joined CORE and SNCC during Freedom Summer in 1964, doing voter registration in Meridian, Mississippi. She moved to Manhattan, where she sought work as a Broadway actress, "a very mistaken ambition" she would later write. Meanwhile, she wrote for periodicals such as *Village Voice, New York Times, Newsday* and *Vogue*, and became a TV news writer for ABC through 1968. She wrote her first book about Shirley Chisholm in 1970. She also wrote *In Our Time: Memoir of a Revolution* in 1999. However, her most important literary contribution was *Against Our Will*, in which she discusses rape as a means perpetuating male dominance by keeping all women in a state of fear. Of the book she wrote: "My purpose in this book has been to give rape its history. Now we must deny its future" (Answers.com 2009).

In 1995, The New York Public Library chose it as one of the 100 most important books of the twentieth century. Since its publication it has been translated into 16 languages.

Today she maintains a website, and continues to write and speak. Her awards include the *Mademoiselle* Achievement Award (1975) and the Women in Communication Matrix Award (1984).

Charlotte Bunch

In the era of the radical feminist, Charlotte Bunch became a major force in articulation of the lesbian-feminism movement. Rita Mae Brown called her "one of the best tactical political minds I have ever encountered." A member of both DC Women's Liberation and the Furies Collective, she wrote the inaugural essay for the Furies Collective newsletter, a piece called *Lesbians in Revolt*. She states the case for lesbianism by writing, "The Lesbian is in revolt because she defines herself in terms of women and rejects the male definitions of how she should feel, act, look and live." She referenced the term "woman identified woman" from the Radicalesbians of New York, recognizing the profound threat that the lesbian ideology presented to the male-dominated culture, stating,

> Lesbianism puts women first while the society declares the male supreme . . . the lesbian has recognized that giving support and love to men over women perpetuates the system that oppresses her . . . for the Lesbian or heterosexual woman, there is no individual solution to oppression . . . (Bunch 1972, 1).

Bunch declared that lesbianism is more than a sexual preference, but a political choice, and emphasized the persecution of the gay woman perpetuated by society: "The Lesbian . . . has little vested interest in maintaining the present political system since all of its institutions—church, state, media, health, schools . . . work to keep her down" (Bunch 1972, 3).

Bunch also recognized in practical terms the perceived economic threat of the self-reliant woman—whether lesbian or straight: "Capitalism cannot absorb large numbers of women demanding stable employment, decent salaries, and refusing to accept their traditional job exploitation" (Bunch 1972, 4).

Born on October 13, 1944, in North Carolina, Charlotte Bunch grew up in Artesia, New Mexico. In 1966 she graduated magna cum laude from Duke University, with a bachelor of arts degree in history and political science. She conducted her graduate research through a fellowship with the Institute for Policy Study in Washington, DC.

She wrote *The New Women: A Motive Anthology on Women's Liberation* (1970). She edited the feminist journal, *The Quest: A Female Journal*, and has written numerous articles on feminist subjects.

She is a professor at Rutgers University in New Jersey, with the Bloustein School of Planning and Public Policy. She founded The Center for Women's Global Leadership (Global Center) at Douglas College, Rutgers University. From there, she continued to campaign for the rights of women and for freedom of sexual orientation, but now on a global scale. She addressed the United Nations Conference on Women's Rights, Vienna, 1993, declaring, "We want people to realize that much of the rape in the world today is a form of terrorism."

Charlotte Bunch was inducted into the National Women's Hall of Fame in 1996, and received the "Women Who Made a Difference Award" from the National Council on Research on Women in 2000.

Mary Daly

Mary Daly was a fiery radical feminist theologian who spent her life challenging both the patriarchal structure and theology of not only the Roman Catholic Church, but most of the world's religious system. In her groundbreaking and controversial works—*The Church and the Second Sex* (1968), and *Beyond God the Father* (1973)—this theology professor at Boston College declared the woman's movement a spiritual movement. Initially a reformist, Daly felt the oppression of women is upheld by most organized religion, and proposed a feminist-based theology.

Mary Daly was born on October 16, 1928, in Schenectady, New York. She was raised by her parents Ann Catherine (Morse) and Frank X. Daly in Catholic institutions, emerging as an undergraduate at College of Saint Rose in Albany, New York, in 1940. She earned her masters degree in English in 1952 at Catholic University of America. She obtained her PhD in religion from St. Mary's College, Notre Dame in 1954. She taught philosophy at Cardinal Cushing College in Brookline, Massachusetts, from 1954–1959.

In the 1950s, no American universities allowed women into graduate theology programs, so in 1959 she sojourned to University of Fribourg in Switzerland where she received two more degrees: a doctorate in sacred theology, and a PhD in philosophy. In 1966, Daly joined the faculty at Boston College as an assistant professor of theology. She remained at Boston College for 33 years during a brilliant and tumultuous career.

Between 1969 and 1973, Daly rejected the concept of church reform in favor of theological revolution. Daly took aim at male supremacy of organized Christianity in her first two books. In *The Church and the Second Sex*, she used the ideas of Simone de Beauvoir to critique the oppressive nature of the patriarchal church. She asserted that separate and different education for women in the church kept women as inferior. The church encouraged esteem of the women to be derived completely from the relationship of her husband, such as in the writings of Pope Pius XII, who seemed to see women as essentially baby machines:

> A cradle consecrates the mother of the family; and more cradles sanctify and glorify her before her husband and children, before Church and homeland. The mother who complains because a new child presses against her bosom seeking nourishment at her breast is foolish, ignorant of herself, and unhappy . . . Even the pains that, since original sin, a mother has to suffer to give birth to her child only draw tighter the bond that binds them: she loves it the more, the more pain it has cost (Daly 1968, 114).

She saw his writings as a sadistic statement from an old man who obviously has never experienced anything close to childbirth. Daly continued through the book to identify the injustice toward women featured through Biblical and church history.

The publication of *The Church and the Second Sex* almost derailed her career at Boston College. The administration at Boston College denied Daly tenure and briefly fired her in 1969—partially because of the book, and partially because the administration demanded she admit men into classes or retire. But due to overwhelming student protests, she was reinstated, promoted, and given tenure—but all without much communication and reconciliation from the male Jesuit administration. Written at the time of the Second Vatican Council, which reportedly would hail great progressive changes within the Catholic Church, Daly said, "The experience of being fired for writing *The Church and the Second Sex* introduced me to the idea that it's not going to change."

In *Beyond God the Father: Toward a Philosophy of Women's Liberation* (1973), Daly presented her gynocentric theology by challenging nearly every patriarchal precept of Western civilization. She advanced the notion of becoming versus being, while humorously looking at what she saw as the absurd patriarchy of the church.

> The females, in the terrifying, exhilarating experience of becoming rather than reflecting, would discover that they too have been infected by the dynamics of the Mirror World . . . Looking inside

for something there, they would be confused by what first would appear to be an endless Hall of Mirrors. What to copy? What model to imitate? Where to look? What is a mere mirror to do? But wait—How could mere mirror even frame such a question? The question itself is the beginning of an answer that keeps unfolding itself (Daly 1973, 197).

She saw herself as a pirate of patriarchy, plundering gems of knowledge stolen from women by patriarchy, and smuggling back to women plundered treasure. She cultivated in women courage to sin—the Indo-European root "to be." Her purpose became "seeing, naming, and dissecting the structures of patriarchy in order to liberate women's minds, bodies, and spirits from its oppression" (Bridle 1, 2009).

Throughout her career, Daly offered ideas that often breached the limits of merely controversial. She concluded that all religions oppress and objectify women. She saw sexism in language as a stumbling block to the explanation of female spirituality. Use of language—that is, he, mankind, God the father, and so forth—was political, and a way of keeping women subjective. She supported drastic reduction of proportion of males in the population, and saw homosexuality as a threat to the nuclear family, which keeps women subjective.

Mary Daly died on January 3, 2010, in Gardner, Massachusetts, at the age of 81.

Dana Densmore

Dana Densmore became one of the true warriors in the radical feminist movement. Intellectual and dedicated, as a founding member of Boston Women's Liberation, which became known as Cell 16, she became an advocate for celibacy, self defense, and women's liberation. In 1968 she cowrote the theoretical feminist journal *No More Fun and Games*, which challenged long-held societal beliefs about women and their need for sexuality, relationship with men and other women, and powerful stance in the world. "We were not promising men that the liberation of women was going to be to their advantage; on the contrary, we were going to end the game playing they found so appealing" (Densmore 1998, 79–80).

Dana Densmore grew up in a household steeped in the Leftist Marxian philosophy. Her mother, Donna Allen, was an antiwar activist and founder of Women Strike for Peace. Her sister—Martha Leslie Allen—went on to write *The History of Women's Media*. She supported and inspired Dana's early acceleration toward the women's movement. Densmore earned her bachelor of arts degree at St. John's College in Annapolis, 1965

Following in her mother's footsteps, Dana became active in the resistance to the draft for the Vietnam War. But she became disillusioned with the role the men of the New Left expected the women to play:

> ... the weekly dinner meetings of The Resistance were exercises in self laceration for the women ... we cooked and cleaned up while the men bonded, strategized, and postured ... The girls enjoined to say yes to the boys who said no ... Though of equal intelligence and thoughtfulness, and equal commitment, we had no legitimacy as a part of the struggle ... (Densmore 1998, 73).

Like many of the women of the Left, Densmore found no support for the exploration of her own liberation, and in fact was derided as selfish in any attempt. She began to explore the burgeoning women's movement and, in May 1968, started corresponding with Jo Freeman, aka Joreen, the editor of Chicago's *Voice for Women's Liberation Movement*.

In July of 968, she attended a workshop given by Roxanne Dunbar on Valerie Solana's *SCUM Manifesto*. Exhilarated by the electric *SCUM Manifesto*, Densmore and Dunbar began to commiserate and collaborate about the need for a women's liberation group in Boston. They went on to found Cell 16 in the summer of 1968.

Asserting that "we shall not fight on the enemy's grounds," Dunbar believed all women were oppressed by men, the family was the cornerstone of male supremacy, and that women were the proletariat of the family. She also asserted that women's behavior was due to sexual conditioning, not material condition.

Dunbar advocated that women's interest in sex, fashion, makeup, and children indicated collaboration with the oppressive system. Densmore actively began training in martial arts by 1968, suggesting,

"Most women are afraid of physical conflict because they have been brought up as 'women'" (Davidson 1969, 1). She said women must be unconditioned from believing in their own inferiority. She preached celibacy and karate to foster self-sufficiency. She kindled the interest in wearing khaki pants, work shirts, combat boots, and short hair. Densmore became a warrior in the battle of the sexes.

When Cell 16 disbanded in 1973, Densmore pursued careers in teaching, publishing, and computer technology. She worked as systems programmer at Massachusetts Institute of Technology (MIT), and for both NASA's Apollo Project and Space Shuttle. She wrote "A Year of Living Dangerously: 1968" for *The Feminist Memoir Project (1998)*. In 1981 she joined the faculty at St. John's College in Santa Fe, where she met William H. Donahue, director of laboratories. With Donahue in 1994, she founded Green Lion Press.

Roxanne Dunbar

Roxanne Dunbar emerged from poverty in central Oklahoma to become a founder of one of most prominent groups in the radical feminist era, Cell 16 of Boston. Throughout her life she held a particular affinity for women disenfranchised both for their gender and their culture.

Roxy Amanda Dunbar was born in San Antonio, Texas, and raised in Piedmont, Oklahoma. Raised Southern Baptist, Dunbar was the "Okie" progeny of Scotch-Irish father Moyer Heywood Dunbar, and half-Indian mother Louise Edna Curry. She was the youngest of four, with Laurence, Hank, and Vera born before her. Dunbar wrote, "I don't know for sure my tribal background, but most likely Cherokee. My maternal grandmother definitely was (American) Indian or part-Indian but died when my mother was 4, and no one ever wanted to talk about her or maybe didn't know her background. Colonialism creates many orphans" (Roxanne Dunbar 2009).

Roxy was steeped in the Leftist traditions of anarchism and socialism. Her grandfather, Emmett Victor Dunbar, was an organizer for the Industrial Workers of the World (IWW) and the Oklahoma Socialist Party. Reared in a poor family by an alcoholic mother who grew more violent with age, Roxy finally ran away to Oklahoma City at 16, marrying a rich white boy named Jimmy at 18. She would eventually divorce him, and lose custody of her daughter Michelle (with whom she has since been reunited).

Roxanne migrated to the West Coast, to study history at San Francisco State University, eventually (1974) receiving her PhD in history—Latin American focus—at UCLA. She planned to travel to Cuba via Mexico, to follow the revolutionary communist regime of Castro and Guevara. But the assassinations of Martin Luther King and Bobby Kennedy—and particularly the attempted assassination of artist Andy Warhol—sidetracked her, and she ended up in Boston. Maintaining her New Left ties she became active in SDS, the Weather Underground, and the African National Congress.

Dunbar seemed particularly fascinated with the attack of Valerie Solanas on the iconic Andy Warhol. She saw Solanas act "as a signal that a women's liberation movement had begun in the United States" (Dunbar 1998, 93). She visited Solanas at the New York Women's House of Detention, hoping to find a superhero woman advocate. Instead, saw a Solanas confused and unstable, a woman on the verge of mental crisis, facing a sanity hearing. Nevertheless, she was enthralled with Solanas' *SCUM (Society for Cutting Up Men) Manifesto* (1967), and she remained in Boston to pursue the women's liberation movement. She founded Boston Women's Liberation, which came to be known as Cell 16, the first prominent women's organization to advocate cultural feminism.

Roxanne Dunbar became a visible and forceful leader of Cell 16. She raised eyebrows at her September 1968 debate with Betty Friedan on a local New York television station. Dunbar served as an expert witness in a rape case in Boston, involving a married former call girl raped by a former john, who held a knife to her throat near the Charles River. It was one of the first cases to argue that a wife or even prostitute cannot be forced to have sex against their will. She helped win the case.

Dunbar moved to New Orleans in 1970, to found Socialist Female Rights Union. Always controversial and outspoken in her opinions, she opposed legalized abortion as a path for genocide of blacks, and saw lesbianism as nothing more than a personal solution (Echols 1989, 165).

She completed her PhD at UCLA in 1974. She joined the faculty at California State University, Hayward, teaching in the Native American Studies department. She helped to develop the Department of Ethnic Studies, as well as Women's Studies. Her other books include *The Great Sioux Nation: An Oral History of the Sioux Nation and Its Struggle for Sovereignty* (1977), *Blood on the Border: A Memoir of the Contra War* (2005), and *Growing up Okie* (1997).

Shulamith Firestone

A cofounder of New York Radical Women, New York Radical Feminists, and Redstockings, Shulamith Firestone rocketed like a comet across the sky in the early radical feminist era, with her futuristic socialistic musings on the effect of feminism on the culture. Her book *Dialectic of Sex* (1970) asserted a tremendous influence on radical feminist theory. Then, as she seemed to hit her apex as an important radical feminist thinker, just as suddenly, within about five short years, she faded away from the movement, succumbing to apparent mental illness.

Born in 1945 in Ottawa, Canada, Shulamith Firestone and her family relocated to St. Louis, Missouri. Her older sister Tirzah Firestone became an important progressive rabbi. Shulamith attended Yavney of Telshe Yeshiva, Washington University, and the Art Institute of Chicago. Her younger sister, Laya Firestone Seghi, is now a social worker.

In 1967, while attending the Art Institute of Chicago, Firestone joined the Westside Group. She also became a major player in Chicago Women's Liberation Union. But in October 1967, she moved to New York to help start NYRW. In 1969, as NYRW split between politicos and radicals feminists, Firestone felt the Leftist movement still carried discriminatory practices with it. Disagreements roiled over her leadership style—perceived by some as egotistic and elitist—and also over which brand of feminism would be preached. In February 1969, Firestone and Ellen Willis organized the Redstockings.

Firestone wrote several important essays, including a history of the women's movement in America called "The Women's Rights Movement in the USA," which appeared in *Notes from the First Year*. Firestone recapped the women's movement in America, perhaps as a reminder of the work that had preceded them. Her most important contribution to the feminist movement, however, came with her 1970 publication of *Dialectic of Sex*. In it, Firestone uses the dialectic methods of Engels and Marx, "to trace the development of economic classes to organic causes."

Firestone concluded that the oppressive position of women has been due primarily to biology; pregnancy, childbirth, and subsequent child-rearing make them ultimately dependent on males. (as opposed to Millett, who argued that biology played a small part; it was culture and psychology which supported the oppression.) Firestone wrote that sexual oppression is at the heart of economic oppression, and that the traditional nuclear family was at the heart of both sexual and economic oppression. She asserted that sexual repression keeps the nuclear family intact, creating neurosis and cultural illness. She proposed that Freud's oedipal complex was more about power than sex, and argued that the sexual roles themselves convey a distribution of power. "Marx was onto something more profound than he knew when he observed that the family contained within itself in miniature all the antagonisms that later develop on a wide scale in the society and the state" (Firestone 1970, 12).

Firestone described pregnancy as "barbaric." She compared the act to defecating a pumpkin, and called for the cessation of the practice. She advocated for the intervention of science and technology to alleviate the dependent role, campaigning for human reproduction through laboratories, and artificial wombs. She predicted the advent of sex selection and in vitro fertilization, and promoted unrestricted access to contraception and government-sponsored child care. She also advocated for the abolition of the tyrannical nuclear family and development of community units within socialistic society. These community units would stand at the heart of an alternate system, which supports freedom from the tyranny of reproductive biology, full self determination—including economic—for women and children; total integration of women and children into larger society—feminist socialism rather than wages, and freedom of sexuality for women and children.

After the publication of *Dialectic of Sex*, Shulamith Firestone seemed to virtually disappear from the women's movement. She reportedly suffered from mental illness, which may have manifested itself in some of her later activities in the public eye. She was hospitalized on several occasions. Feminist writer Andrea Dworkin reportedly told British journalist Linda Grant that Firestone was "poor and crazy" and that she rents a room and fills it with clutter. She gets kicked out and moves into another room and fills it with junk.

In 1967 Firestone was the subject of a documentary film, the newest version of which—called *Shulie*, by Elisabeth Subria—was released in 1997. Firestone tried her hand at publishing again in 1998, with the release of *Airless Spaces*.

> Of Shulamith Firestone's current situation, her sister Laya Seghi writes:
> Shulamith has been incommunicado for a number of years already and remains reclusive, continuing to live on the lower east side of NYC as she has done since moving there from Chicago in 1967 . . . she was one of the most extraordinary people I have ever known . . . intense, brilliant, with an acute political sensibility and a tragic personal life (Laya Seghi 2009).

Jo Freeman

Perhaps the most politically oriented of the radical feminists, Jo Freeman is a writer who—under the pen name Joreen—became editor of the *The Voice for Women's Liberation*, the first national women's liberation newsletter, and a producer of numerous important works on the women's movement. However, she was criticized by others in the early feminist movement, who saw her as too individually ambitious. Outspoken and often critical of the movements in which she participated, her personal comportment and success seemed to rankle members of the women's movement.

Jo Freeman was born on August 26, 1945, in Atlanta, Georgia. Her mother, Helen Mitchell Freeman, from Marion County, Alabama, moved to southern California, taught junior high school, dying in 1973. Her father was not around.

Freeman attended Birmingham Junior High School, then Granada Hills High in the San Fernando Valley. She called the University of California at Berkeley—where she earned her bachelor's degree in political science—"her personal liberation." At Berkeley, she became active with Young Democrats and SLATE, as well as the Bay Area Civil Rights Movement. She was arrested for demonstrating at the Sheraton-Palace Hotel and at a Cadillac Dealership, both for job discrimination against African Americans. She was also arrested with eight hundred other students for occupying the administration building at UC Berkeley. Involved in the Free Speech Movement, she wrote her thesis on civil disobedience, but when studying the abolitionist movement of the 19th century, she became convinced the next major movement would be the women's.

In 1964 she traveled to the South to join the SCLC in freedom summer—the only white woman on the field staff. Many of her experiences in the civil rights movement inspired her work as a feminist. However, some claimed her to be a professional agitator and communist sympathizer, and she was sent by the SCLC to Chicago, where she worked with Coretta Scott King.

In Chicago, she got a job as a reporter and editor for a community newspaper called *TORCH*. She confronted the discrimination women faced in journalism, while developing her skills as a writer and photojournalist. While in Chicago, she attended a course on women conducted by Heather Booth and Naomi Weisstein, and helped organize Chicago's first women's liberation group, the West Side Group. She met Shulamith Firestone at the National Conference for New Politics in Chicago on Labor Day Weekend in 1967.

With the advent of the Chicago Women's Liberation Union, she became editor of *The Voice for Women's Liberation.*

Freeman's diligent efforts in feminist and leftist politics became vast and varied. In 1968, Freeman discovered NOW and helped start the Chicago chapter of NOW. In the summers of 1970 and 1971, she hitchhiked in Europe distributing feminist pamphlets. She ran as a delegate for Shirley Chisholm in 1972. In 1974 she shifted membership to the New York City chapter, and to the Washington, DC chapter in 1977.

She earned her PhD in political science from the University of Chicago 1973, and spent four years teaching at the State University of New York. She spent two years at Washington, DC as a Brookings Fellow and as an APSA Congressional Fellow. In 1975, she won $1000 from American Political Science Association. In 1976 attended the Democratic and Republican National Conventions as a reporter for *MS*. In 1982 she earned her JD and joined the New York State Bar in 1983. She opened a private law practice in 1999.

Freeman became renowned for three essays offering insight into the feminist movement, which she penned under the name Joreen. The first, *The Bitch Manifesto (1969)* (see Addendum 4) is a lyrical essay, which expounded on the term used derogatorily toward women who "rudely violate conceptions of proper sex role behavior" (Freeman 1970, 2).

The Bitch Manifesto resounded through the women's movement, because so many members no doubt had become quite familiar with the term in a personal way. Freeman urged "a woman should be proud to declare she is a Bitch, because Bitch is Beautiful" (Freeman 1970, 2).

"The Tyranny of Structurelessness" (1970) first appeared in the New York Radical Women's *Notes from the Third Year*. In response to what she saw as a plethora of leaderless and therefore ineffective groups among the early feminist organizations, she argued that there is no such thing as a structureless group. She asserted that pretending there was allowed responsibility to be shirked and power to be hidden. She claimed that every group had structure, usually based on friendship networks. In absence of democratic structure, these networks make decisions.

Freeman wrote "Trashing: Darkside of Sisterhood" after she left Chicago. It appeared in *MS*. magazine in 1976, reportedly evoking more lettered response than any previous article. The essay denounced what appeared to be a common practice among the feminist groups, which Freeman described as "a particularly vicious form of character assassination which amounts to psychological rape. It is manipulative, dishonest, and excessive . . . it is done to disparage and destroy" (Freeman 1976, 2). She postulated that the penchant for trashing may be a consequence of the inward-turned rage that the women have long felt which only now—in the seemingly relative safety of the women's groups—is pouring out in unhealthy ways.

> . . . the collective cost of allowing trashing to go on as long and as extensively as we have is enormous. We have already lost some of the most creative minds and dedicated activists . . . we have discouraged other feminists from stepping out, out of fear that they, too, would be trashed (Freeman 1976, 8).

Her other writing feats include "What the Hell Is Women's Liberation?" which she wrote for the *Guardian; The Politics of Women's Liberation: A Case Study for an Emerging Social Movement and Its Relation to the Policy Process (McKay 1975);* and *Politics of Women's Liberation (1975).* She also edited five editions of *Women: A Feminist Perspective (1975, 1979, 1984, 1989, 1995).*

Carol Hanisch

Carol Hanisch was a radical feminist active in the Gainesville, Florida, movement, New York Radical Women, and Redstockings. Originally a UPI reporter on civil rights, she gained notoriety for an essay called "The Personal Is Political," which in one stroke validated the personal oppression experiences of women as important issues in the struggle for women's rights. She was also the muse for the 1968 protest of the Miss America Pageant in New York, which served to thrust the women's liberation movement into the national spotlight.

"The Personal Is Political" appeared in New York Radical Women's *Notes from the Second Year* in February of 1969. It began as a memo called "Some Thoughts in Response to Dottie's Thoughts on a Women's Liberation Movement" while she worked for the Southern Conference Educational Fund (SCEF). Edited by Shulamith Firestone and Ann Koedt, it is thought they provided the title.

The essay addressed a primary issue that hovered over the feminist movement: is consciousness-raising a form of political action? In the article, Hanisch wrote that some women argued against consciousness-raising, claiming women were brainwashed and complicit in their own oppression. But Hanisch argued that it is important to recognize the need to fight male supremacy instead of blaming the individual woman for her oppression, and to understand that oppressive situations are not the woman's own fault. "Women are messed over" she said, "not messed up". She asserted that political action and consciousness-raising do not necessarily cancel each other out. "Maybe the answer is not to put down the method of analyzing from personal experiences in favor of immediate action, but to figure out what can be done to make it work" (Hanisch 1969, 4).

Hanisch supported the continuation of consciousness-raising sessions because from them, "I have gotten a political understanding which all my reading, all my "political discussions," all my political action, all my four-odd years in the Movement never gave me." She campaigned to figure out why women have left the Movement "in droves. The obvious reason is that we are tired of being sex slaves and doing shitwork for men whose hypocrisy is so blatant in their political stance of liberation for everybody else" (Hanisch 1998, 198).

Carol Hanisch was born and raised in Iowa, attending Drake University where she majored in journalism. She became a civil rights reporter with United Press International, and then in 1965 volunteered for the civil rights movement, joining SCEF in Gainesville. She moved to New York in 1966, and then became a founding member of New York Radical Women as the group met in the New York SCEF office.

According to her essay in the *Feminist Memoir Project*, Carol Hanisch described how the idea of the Miss America Pageant protest came to her in the summer of 1968, while watching the film *Schmearguntz* with New York Radical Women:

> The idea crept into my head that protesting the pageant in Atlantic City just might be the way to bring the fledgling Women's Liberation Movement into the public arena . . . As Ros Baxandall was to remark later on the David Susskind TV show, "every day in a woman's life is a walking Miss America contest." It seemed just the boat to start rocking (Hanisch 198, 198).

The event put the women's liberation movement on the map for most of the nation. The NYRW drew more members, which also widened the factions between politicos and feminists, and doomed NYRW.

Afterwards, Hanisch expressed some regrets about how the protest was handled. She said "I wrote how the anti-women faction of the protesters detracted from our message that all women are oppressed by beauty standards, even the contestants."

Hanisch later joined the Redstockings, becoming editor of the anthology *Feminist Revolution*. In 1997 she published *Frankly*

Feminist, and wrote the play *Promise and Betrayal*. Hanisch now lives in upstate New York.

Kate Millett

Kate Millett was a member of the New York Chapter of NOW, and of the NYRW. She is best known for turning her Columbia University thesis into the book *Sexual Politics: A Manifesto for Revolution* (1970), a comprehensive critique of patriarchy in Western society and literature. Katherine Murray Millett was born in St. Paul, Minnesota, on September 14, 1934. She was the middle of three daughters conceived by Helen Freely Millett and James Albert Millett. James abandoned the family when Kate was 14. Kate helped with the family by working part-time jobs to support her mother's work.

In 1956 Millett graduated Phi Beta Kappa from the University of Minnesota. A member of Kappa Alpha Theta sorority, she completed her master's degree in English at St. Hilda's College, Oxford University, due to the generosity of a wealthy aunt. She moved to New York from 1959 to 1961, where she learned to paint and sculpt. *Sexual Politics* started as her PhD dissertation at Columbia University.

Millett taught college briefly in North Carolina, and in 1964 she taught at Barnard College, and joined CORE. She spent two years in Tokyo, teaching at Waseda University and working on her sculpture. She married sculptor Fumio Yoshimura in 1965, amicably divorcing him in 1985. By 1967, Millett's art began to attract attention, and she was featured in an exhibit at Judson Gallery in Greenwich Village. In the meantime, she discovered the feminist movement, joining first NOW New York, then NYRW.

At the end of 1970, Millett fully discovered the repression of enforced heterosexuality, as a *Time* magazine article called "Women's Lib: A Second Look" appeared on the newsstands. Apparently meant to discredit the bourgeoning women's movement, the article revealed that Kate Millett was bisexual, and Millett faced public confrontation of her lifestyle. But ultimately, instead of discrediting feminism, the article helped to bring the lesbian component of feminism to surface, where it was supported and explored by other radical feminists.

Kate Millett sometimes became depressed and eventually made several suicide attempts. Her family institutionalized her, the situation of which she explores in *The Looney-Bin Trip* (1990). In 1991, on Britain's Channel 4 television show *After Dark*, she confronted popular English actor Oliver Reed for his chauvinistic behavior—including kissing her on the air. She demanded his departure from the set, and created a sensation.

But Millett is best remembered for intellectual insights offered to the feminist movement. She claimed that sex is a minor need blown out of proportion by men, and that the real lover is the most lucid of persons. She advocated separation from men as a tactic of organizing women, both personally and politically, and pointed out that pornography reinforces male power over women. She stated that male concept or principle has created a chaotic, violent, greedy world, characteristics unknown in matriarchal societies, and antithetical to female principle. She said, "We need an alliance of the two to create cooperation and a truly humanistic society."

Since 1970, the author of *The Prostitution Papers* (1973) has purchased a Christmas tree farm in upstate, New York, which serves as summer sanctuary for female artists.

Robin Morgan

One of the most influential voices and powerful personalities among radical feminists, she was characterized as a "bohemian, radiant, glamour girl." A politico and Yippie entrenched in the antiwar movement, her conversion from the New Left militant to radical feminist reflected the experience of thousands of other women in 60s. She organized media coverage of the 1968 Miss America protest, and was the editor, mentor, and contributor to Jane Alpert's *Mother Right*. A member of NYRW, she also helped to create the Women's International Terrorist Conspiracy from Hell (WITCH). Morgan would plead for feminists to search for connections, and tried to mitigate the divisive chasm between straight and gay women. A founder of *MS.* magazine and editor of Grove Press, Morgan edited *Sisterhood Is Powerful* (1970) and wrote the essay "*Going too Far (Goodbye to All That)*," Morgan's farewell to the radical male left.

Born Robin Evonne on January 29, 1941, in Lake Worth, Florida, her parents were divorced before she was born. Robin grew up in Mount Vernon, New York, raised by her mother Faith Berkeley Morgan and a maternal aunt. Although she grew up in an "apostate Jewish household," she became a "wiccan atheist." She first met her father at 18, and she characterized her subsequent meetings with him as "infrequent and disappointing."

A child actress, she played youngest child Dagmar Hansen during the first year of the television series *Mama* in 1949. She attended Columbia University from 1956 to 1959, she married Kenneth Pitchford in 1962 at the age of 21 (and divorced him in 1990). She had one child, a son named Blake.

In the mid-1960s, Morgan became active with the antiwar left and a member of the Youth International Party with Abbie Hoffman and Paul Grassner. She worked as a freelance editor and writer for numerous New Left journals, including *Liberation, Rat, Win,* and *The Guardian.*

But as tensions over sexism arose within the New Left movement, Morgan began leaning toward a feminist alternative, believe radical feminism to be an important component of a larger revolution. She organized demonstrations to free Valerie Solanas in 1965.

She helped to create WITCH, using public street theater tactics to call attention to sexism.

She was a founder of *MS.* magazine, continuing as contributing editor in late 1970s, and editor-in-chief from 1989 to 1994. She has been an international contributing editor for the magazine since 1993.

She served as a special consultant on global feminism in the late 1980s, and has served on the boards of Feminist Women's Health Network, National Battered Women's Refuge Network, National Network of Rape Crisis Centers, and Women against Pornography. Morgan is founder of the Sisterhood Is Global Institute, and cofounder of The Women's Media Center.

About the women's movement, she once was stated:

> I do not make the argument that women are inherently more peaceable, nurturing, or altruistic than men. (For one thing, this permits men the laziest of justifications for their own behavior.) Yet it is undeniable that history is a record of most women acting peaceably

and most men acting belligerently—to a point to where the capacity for belligerence is regarded as an essential ingredient of manhood and the proclivity for conciliation is thought largely a quality of women (Morgan, 1989).

Vivian Rothstein

One of the "gang of four" from Chicago, Vivian Rothstein became the first staff person for the CWLU. Rothstein grew up a cultural outsider who became a veteran of the New Left movements. She was a member of the SDS before helping to activate the women's movement in Chicago. She advocated a single uniform to combat consumerism, and married a "New Left heavy," Richard Rothstein. She belonged to the SNCC, the Council of Federated Organizations, and the Free Speech Movement before joining the Westside Group and the CWLU.

Vivian Leburg was born in New York City in 1945, to Margot Johanna and Werner Chaim Leburg. Vivian's parents split up when she was born but never divorced. Vivian was raised in Studio City in southern California, where she and her mother worked, and lived in a house owned by her uncle. Since they were descendents of German-Jewish refugees, Jewish persecution and the holocaust cast a deep shadow over the household. There was always worry about "they could come and get us at any time" which created dichotomy of respect and suspicion of authority. "It caused me to identify with people on the outside who are singled out for oppressive and discriminatory treatment," she said. From early in her life, Vivian herself felt like an outsider, and learned to identify with the disenfranchised. Her best friend in school was a girl of Japanese American heritage. Rothstein's older sister—Barbara Joan Algaze—now lives in Los Angeles.

Vivian graduated from Hollywood High School 1963, and came to UC Berkeley to attend college. At Berkeley, she found a job as a tutor of blind girl from Texas who hated blacks, even though she had never actually seen one. This inflamed Vivian's own sense of disenfranchisement, and motivated her to join the fight for others who felt left out. She joined the demonstration against Lucky's Markets for discriminatory hiring practices, and was arrested for protesting at San Francisco's Auto Row Demo for the same issue.

She also joined the Free Speech movement. She traveled to the South for Mississippi Summer, landing in jail in Jackson, Mississippi, in 1965 for marching on the sidewalk with no permit. She also joined the SDS in Oakland and Chicago. In 1967 Vivian traveled to Vietnam as part of an American peace delegation to observe targets of American bombing. In Vietnam, she met with members of the Vietnamese Women's Union, which had been developed as an instrument by which women could advocate for their civil rights. She said her meeting with these women had a profound impact on her and her interest in building an independent women's movement in the United States.

Upon returning from Vietnam, Rothstein came to Chicago and joined the Westside Group with the others of the Gang of Four, including Amy Kesselman, Naomi Weisstein, and Heather Tobis Booth. She became the first (unpaid) staff person for the CWLU in 1968. She worked to establish the CWLU office, newsletter, and membership list.

She lived with her husband Richard in the Magnolia Street commune in the north side of Chicago until 1973. The commune proved to be an experiment in group cohabitation, and a challenge—both positive and detrimental—to Rothstein's previously held notions of workable relationships. Vivian has two children: Jesse, 35, is an economist working for the Council of Economic Advisors in the Obama administration; and Leah, 33, works for a consulting firm advising governments in the development of affordable and sustainable housing.

After leaving Chicago in 1974, Rothstein has continued her efforts for social justice. She worked with the American Friends Service Committee and with Planned Parenthood. She also worked for 10 years in Santa Monica, California, with homeless and battered women and children. She now represents the Hotel Workers International Union, advocating for livable wages for service workers, the majority of whom are women.

Kathie Sarachild

An early founding member of NYRW and Redstockings, Sarachild is credited with coining the phrase "Sisterhood Is Powerful" in 1968, which became a rallying cry for the women's movement. She wrote the article "Program for Feminist Consciousness-raising," becoming a major architect of consciousness-raising and one of the most vocal proponents of the feminist line.

She was born Kathie Amatniek in 1943, but assumed her matrilineal name Sarachild in 1968. She was raised in a left-leaning, lower middle class upbringing. Her mother was an adult education teacher, who taught English as a second language classes, and advocated for equal opportunities for women in education.

Amatniek attended Harvard University, becoming editor of the Harvard *Crimson* and a member of the Harvard peace group TOCSIN. She became an organizer of the Summer Voter Registration Project in 1964 with the SNCC.

Sarachild cofounded the New York Feminist newspaper *Woman's World*. In 1968 she took active roles in both the Jeannette Rankin Parade's "burial of traditional womanhood" and the Miss America Protest.

In November 1968 she gave a presentation at the First National Women's Liberation Conference at Lake Villa, Illinois. The workshop was called "A Program for Feminist Consciousness-Raising," later compiled into an article called "Consciousness-Raising: A Radical Weapon."

Consciousness-raising was a process that became important within the NYRW and other radical feminist groups. In the talk, Sarachild quoted Stokely Carmichael who urged, "Go fight your own oppressors." Consciousness-raising was seen as both a method for arriving at the truth and a means for action and organizing, once "our experience is finally verified and clarified." Sarachild also referenced Malcolm X, who wrote, "If you give people a thorough understanding of what it is that confronts them, and the basic causes that produce it, they'll create their own program; and when the people create a program you get action" (Sarachild 1997). Sarachild was convinced that women had to get clear through consciousness-raising about the exact nature of what confronted them, before they could decide on what action they wanted to take to address it.

She currently serves as a director of Redstockings Women's Liberation Archives in Action.

Valerie Solanas

Although never playing a pivotal organizational role in the women's liberation movement, nevertheless Valerie Solanas became a cause célèbre of the radical feminist movement, expressing the deep rage that many women in the movement felt about the culture of oppression and discrimination surrounding them. Through her 1967 treatise *The SCUM Manifesto*, Solanas unleashed a tirade against the male dominated society and against men themselves. With her opening words, Solanas lets loose a torrent of rage, frustration, and despair about the society women find themselves surrounded by:

> Life in this society being, at best, an utter bore and no aspect of society being at all relevant to women, there remains to civic-minded, responsible, thrill-seeking females only to overthrow the government, eliminate the money system, institute complete automation and destroy the male sex ... The male is a biological accident: the Y (male) gene is an incomplete X (female) gene, that is, it has an incomplete set of chromosomes. In other words, the male is an incomplete female, a walking abortion, aborted at the gene stage (Solanas 1967, 1).

For 17 pages, Solanas unleashes this diatribe against the male gender under the guise of the leader of a fictional radical organization called SCUM (Society of Cutting Up Men). She vengefully examines the effect the Y chromosome has had on such varied social topics as money, marriage, prostitution, fatherhood, mental illness, love, and war: "Since he has no compassion or ability to empathize or identify, proving his manhood is worth an endless amount of mutilation and suffering and endless number of lives ... " (Solanas 1967, 2).

The *Manifesto* struck a nerve with women within and out the movement, particularly when Solanas seemed to take the rage she vented in the *Manifesto*, and turned it outward toward a male target. On June 3, 1968, she shot artist and producer Andy Warhol, because she accused him of stealing a play that she had asked him to produce. Almost instantly Solanas became something of a mythical hero advocate, with her *Manifesto* becoming her creed. Roxanne Dunbar identified with Solanas' rage, concluding that Solanas's act was "a signal that a women's liberation movement had begun in the United States" (Dunbar 1998, 93). Ti-Grace Atkinson called her "the first outstanding champion of women's rights."

Solanas's childhood seemed to provide sufficient justification for her rage. Born on April 9, 1936, in Ventnor City, New Jersey, Valerie Jean Solanas was the daughter of Louis and Dorothy Bondo Solanas. Reportedly her father sexually molested her, and her parents divorced in the 1940s. When Dorothy moved to Washington, DC to remarry, Valerie repeatedly disobeyed her parents and refused to stay in Catholic high school. Her grandfather reportedly beat her. She left home at age 15, dating a sailor who impregnated her. She still managed to graduate from high school, and enrolled at the University of Maryland at College Park. She also did a year of graduate work at the University of Minnesota.

However, after college Solanas had to panhandle, and turned to prostitution to pay her bills. She moved around, finally landing in Greenwich Village in 1966. There, she wrote the play *Up Your Ass*, which would prove a turning point in her life.

In 1967 she approached Andy Warhol at his studio The Factory in New York. She asked Warhol to produce the play; Warhol reportedly seemed to like it, but also thought it was so pornographic that he suspected it was a set up by law enforcement. He never produced the play, never got back to Solanas, and never returned the script to her.

At the same time, Solanas wrote *The SCUM Manifesto*, selling copies of it on the streets, and showing the manuscript to Maurice Girodias at Olympia Press. In May of 1967, Solanas demanded her script back, which apparently Warhol had lost. Solanas began harassing him on the phone, demanding money for her script.

Meanwhile, Solanas's celebrity status increased. She appeared in a couple of Warhol films, and she continued to write. She was interviewed by the Village Voice in an article entitled "Scum Goddess: a Winter Memory of Valerie Solanas," which would not be published until after June 3, 1968. She was also interviewed on Alan Burke's TV talk show. During the interview she refused to censor herself, compelling Burke to walk off the air. In the meantime, Maurice Girodias agreed to pay for a novel Solanas would write based on the *SCUM Manifesto*, if she would give him her next writing and other writings.

Solanas interpreted this to mean Girodias would own everything she ever wrote, and assumed she had been ripped off by both Girodias and Warhol.

Finally, her rage simmered out of control. She shot Warhol on June 3, 1968, was imprisoned in June of 1969, and was finally released in 1971. By 1987, Solanas ended up in northern California. On April 26, 1988, she died alone in an SRO hotel in the Tenderloin district of San Francisco at the age of 52. She reportedly had a drug problem, had been working as a prostitute, and reportedly died of emphysema and pneumonia.

Barbara Winslow

Barbara Winslow made headlines in 1968 when she confronted a Playboy Bunny on "Men's Day" at the University of Washington at Seattle. Cofounder of Women's Liberation in Seattle, Winslow was one of the major players in bringing the ideologies of the radical feminists to the west coast.

Born in 1945 in the Westchester Suburb in Scarsdale, New York, Barbara Winslow remembers being reviled by her classmates as one of two persons who supported Adlai Stevenson for President in 1952. She also remembers being roundly booed in a class debate for expressing opposition to death penalty. Her mother Luella LaMer Slaner was a graduate in political science and history at Wellesley College. Luella was a talented amateur golfer, and reportedly gave up tennis because she was better than her husband, but eventually became better than him in golf as well. Luella gave up political ambition for home life; she wanted to go into the foreign service in the State Department, but instead met and married Alfred Slaner, an executive in hosiery and women's apparel.

Barbara Slaner was brought up in a privileged and liberal household. Her mother was active in the League of Women Voters, the Scarsdale Planning Commission, and the PTA. Both parents helped found the first Planned Parenthood in Scarsdale. Her parents were very open and supportive about abortion, and Barbara developed strong opinions on abortion as well. She actually underwent an abortion in Europe and said the process was easier than in the United

States, but still "painful and humiliating." As ever, women with connections could get abortions, but it became much more difficult for the middle class and poor.

The middle of three daughters, Barbara confessed to be an "alienated mess of contradictions" at Scarsdale High School, seeking at the same time the cheerleader and beatnik crowds. She picketed Woolworths during the lunch-counter sit-ins, and protested the Bay of Pigs Crisis in Cuba. She argued a lot with her parents about life issues as her grades fell. She graduated from a private high school, attended Antioch College, and spent a year and a half in London at Leeds University. Winslow went on to get a bachelor's degree and PhD in history at the University of Washington. She also read *The Feminine Mystique*, which provided her first serious look at "the Women question."

Barbara married her college sweetheart Cal Winslow in 1967. He became a big name among the Seattle New Left community, joining the faculty at the University of Washington, Seattle. Opposed to the Vietnam War, he received a National Defense Education Award Fellowship (NDEA).

In 1966, Winslow attended a series on Women in U.S. Society, sponsored by a Trotskyist group called the Freedom Socialist Party (FSP) and conducted by civil rights activist Gloria Martin. There Winslow met Susan Stern, a University of Washington social work graduate and member of the FSP, along with UW Economics Professor Judith Shapiro. In November of 1967, Stern hosted a meeting in her apartment with Winslow, Shapiro, Martin, and Clara Fraser, who banded together to form the Seattle Radical Women. This became Winslow's first of many sojourns into the political fray without her husband. Seattle Radical Women would begin a 40-year history of championing the disenfranchised in the Pacific Northwest.

Winslow stated that unlike on the east coast, the women's movement seemed to develop with the support of the SDS in Seattle. This seems to coincide with the progressive history of the west, where the acceptance of women in leadership roles took a much earlier societal hold than in the east. Furthermore, the sharp division between politicos and feminists in the women's movement did not seem so prominent in Seattle.

Winslow's personal introduction to the oppression of women within the medical industry came in June of 1968, a month after the

Men's Day melee. After a lump was discovered on her breast, her doctor told her she needed a radical mastectomy, but he also told her she had to get husband's consent. His reasoning: "Because women are too emotionally and irrationally tied to their breasts" (Winslow 1998, 229). This outraged Winslow, but she had no alternative. Her husband signed the form that "gave him control over my breasts." Fortunately, the biopsy showed there was no malignancy, except perhaps a sexist malignancy in the minds of the medical establishment (Winslow 1998, 229).

While in Seattle, she campaigned to legalize abortion, in particular around Referendum 20, which was the first and only time in the United States that a popular referendum legalized abortion. She helped found the women's studies programs at the University of Washington and was the first Professor of Women's Studies at Seattle Central Community College.

Winslow moved to Cleveland, Ohio in 1973, where she remained active in Radical Left feminist politics. She was a founding member of the Coalition of Labor Unions and an officer in the Cleveland Coalition of Union Women as well as in the Cleveland Pro-Choice Network. She was also a founding member and officer of the Left feminist Reproductive Rights National Network (R2N2). She also was a professor of women's studies at Cuyahoga Community College.

Barbara Winslow is now an associate professor of Adolescence and Women's Studies at Brooklyn College. Her first book, *Sylvia Pankhurst: Sexual Politics and Political Activism*, was published in 1996, and she is working on a history of the women's movement in Seattle. She is the founder of the Shirley Chisholm Project of Brooklyn Women's Activism: 1945 to the Present.

Naomi Weisstein

Naomi Weisstein may have been the Loki of the radical feminists. She utilized her skills as a comedian and a musician to raise the consciousness about feminism among men and women. She then turned around and displayed her knowledge and experience as an experimental psychologist to write the brilliant "Kinder, Kuche, Kirche as Scientific Law: Psychology Constructs the Female." Perhaps the era's premiere exposition female psychology, "Psychology Constructs the Female" has been reprinted 42 times in six different languages since it was first published by New England Free Press in 1968.

Born in 1939 in New York City, Naomi Weisstein is the daughter of concert pianist Mary Wenk, and Samuel Weisstein. She graduated Phi Beta Kappa with a BA from Wellesley College in 1961, earning her PhD in psychology at Harvard University in 1964. She showed her flair for the dramatic early, when she protested at Harvard's Lamont Library in 1962. At the time the library was open to males only, as it was felt that women in the library would prove to much of a "distraction" to the serious young men. True to form, she and some friends reported showed up at the library wearing skin-tight leotards, and playing clarinet, tambourines, and trumpet—apparently to make sure all understood what a true distraction meant.

After meeting husband Jesse Lemisch, who obtained a teaching position at the University of Chicago, the couple moved to Chicago, where they joined SDS and CORE. In 1967 Weisstein helped to form the Chicago Westside Group, and then the CWLU in 1969.

In "Psychology Constructs the Female," Weisstein asserted that psychology had nothing to say about what women want, need, or like, because the psychology of women was not known. She contradicted the assumption that human behavior rests on an individual and inner dynamic, and pointed out the inadequacy of such a position without looking at the social context.

A biting humorist, Weisstein began honing her talents as a comedian under the inspiration of the mercurial Lenny Bruce. She became one of the earliest feminist stand-up comedians, particularly known in the 1970s for her routine "Saturday Night Special—Salute to Rape." Her cartoons have appeared in *The Voice of the Women's Liberation Movement, The New University Conference Newsletter* (1969), *The Rogers' Spark* (1970), and other periodicals.

By 1970, disillusioned by the direction in which she felt the CWLU was headed, she founded the Chicago Women's Liberation Rock Band. A classically and jazz-trained pianist, Weisstein and the band toured the northeast and brought consciousness-raising to another level, enjoying remarkable success for three years.

Weisstein became a professor of psychology at SUNY Buffalo, and has written more than 60 articles in such journals as *Science, Vision Research., Psychological Review,* and the *Journal of Experimental Psychology.* In 1982, she was diagnosed with Chronic Fatigue Immune Dysfunction (CFIDS), which has relegated her to her home ever since.

Works Cited

Alpert, Jane, *Mother Right: A New Feminist Theory, MS. magazine,* 1974, 2–3, 6, 8, 11–12.

"An Informal Bio, Susan Brownmiller," 2009, http:// www.answers.com/topic/susan-brownmiller.

Bunch, Charlotte, "Lesbians in Revolt," *The Furies,* January 1972, 1, 3–4.

Davidson, Sara, "An Oppressed Majority Demands Its Rights," *Life Magazine,* 1969, 1–2.

Ceballos, Jaqueline Michot, *Interview with Rosalyn Fraad Baxandall,* Cambridge: The Radcliffe Institute for Advanced Study, 1991, 44, 63.

Daly, Mary, *The Church and the Second Sex,* New York: Harper & Row, 1968, 114.

Daly, Mary, *Beyond God the Father: Toward a Philosophy of Women's Liberation,* Boston: Beacon Press, 1973, 20.

Bridle, Susan, "No Man's Land," *EnlightenNext Magazine,* www.enlightennext.org/magazine/j16/daly.asp, 1.

Densmore, Dana, "A Year of Living Dangerously," *Feminist Memoir Project: Voices from Women's Liberation,* New York: Three Rivers Press (Crown Publishers), 1998, 73, 79–80.

Dunbar, Roxanne, e-mail message to the author, November 8, 2009.

Dunbar, Roxanne, "Outlaw Woman: Chapters from a Feminist Memoir in Progress," *Feminist Memoir Project, Voices from Women's Liberation,* New York: Three Rivers Press (Crown Publishers), 1998.

Echols, Alice, *Daring to Be Bad, Radical Feminism in America, 1967–1975,* Minneapolis, University of Minnesota Press, 1989, 165.

Firestone, Shulameth, *The Dialectic of Sex,* New York: William Morrow and Company, Inc. 1970, 12.

Freeman, Jo, "The BITCH Manifesto," *Notes from the Second Year,* 1972, 2.

Freeman, Jo, "Trashing: Darkside of Sisterhood," 1975, *MS. Magazine,* 1976, 8.

Hanisch, Carol, "The Personal Is Political," *Notes from the Second Year,* 1969, 4.

Hanisch, Carol, "Two Letters from the Women's Liberation Movement," *Feminist Memoir Project, Voices from Women's Liberation,* New York: Three Rivers Press (Crown Publishers), 1998, 198.

Morgan, Robin, The Demon Lover: On the Sexuality of Terrorism, 1989, http:// en.wikipedia.org/wiki/Robin_Morgan.

Sachs, Andrea, "Rita Mae Brown: Loves Cats, Hates Marriage," *Time Magazine,* March.

Sarachild, Kathie, "Consciousness-Raising: A Radical Weapon," 1978, http://scriptorium.lib.duke.edu/wlm/fem/sarachild.html.
Seghi, Laya, e-mail to the author, September 7, 2009.
Solanas, Valerie, *The SCUM Manifesto*, 1–2.
Ter, Cheryl, "Jane: Abortion and the Underground," Women News Section, Chicago Tribune Online, September 1999, 2–3.
Winslow, Barbara, *Feminist Memoir, Feminist Memoir Project: Voices from Women's Liberation*, New York: Three Rivers Press (Crown Publishers), 1998, 229.

Glossary

Bra-Burners: A description often used by the media to describe radical feminists. It was first raised during the 1968 Miss America Protest in Atlantic City, and became permanently associated with feminism—even though not one bra was burned during the protest.

Consciousness-raising: A group exercise employed by many radical feminist organizations to raise the level of awareness of their own oppression. Women would share their most private thoughts and feelings about their own experiences of male oppression, and come to realize that their experiences were political as well as personal. The practice was often assailed by more action-oriented feminists, who felt such contemplations to be a waste of time.

Cultural Feminism: An offshoot of radical feminist thought that sought to create a culture featuring female-led institutions, where women would develop and flourish separate from the patriarchal society. Cultural feminism assumed that the experiences of women were essentially similar, particularly in relation to men, and their values were superior to men. Critics contended that cultural feminism was a panacea, which distracted women from the struggle to create a new American political and economic system.

Far Left: A term used to describe the most liberal/radical end of the American political spectrum. The Far Left has historically been comprised of abolitionists, communists, socialists, populists, suffragists, anarchists, civil rights advocates, and the antiwar activists.

Lavender Menace: A term used to describe the hazards of acknowledging the lesbian contingent within the feminist movement. Lavender was a color often associated with the lesbian faction. Although the term was attributed to Betty Friedan, it is not clear if she ever actually used it. Susan Brownmiller had claimed that Friedan had used the term "Lavender Herring" instead. At the Second Congress to Unite Women in 1969, a group called the Radicalesbians donned T-shirts reading "Lavender Menace" to challenge feminism's homophobia.

Liberal Feminism: A type of feminist thought which sought to bring about reforms that would empower women within the existing American society which would be neither destroyed or divided. Liberal feminism was generally more inclusive but less militant than either radical or cultural feminism. Unlike radical or cultural feminism, liberal feminism sought an equal partnership with men, including women more fully in the mainstream of society, and ending all forms of sexual discrimination.

New Left: The new manifestation of the Far Left, post–World War II. The New Left was comprised of the socialist, antiwar, and civil rights activists, radicals born on college campuses amidst the apathy of the Ungeneration.

New Right: A new wave of conservatism brought about in the 1970s and 1980s, energized in part from the passage of the ERA, and the decision of Roe v. Wade. The New Right engendered support for American institutions and "family values" perceived by conservatives as threatened by values and lifestyles supported by the feminism. The New Right often drew its strength for conservative, fundamental, and orthodox religious institutions.

Old Left: The Far Left of the pre–World War II era. This includes what is known as the Lyrical Left during the heyday of socialism prior to World War I, and the communist contingent which arose during the Depression.

Politico: A term used to describe those feminists closely tied to the New Left, who believed the liberation of women was tied to the larger liberation of the American people from the patriarchal, capitalistic system. Politicos sought women's liberation through political and social action, rather than consciousness-raising. The politicos saw the target of change as not men, but the capitalistic system which oppressed women.

Radical Feminism: A type of feminism which sought to overthrow the basic capitalistic, patriarchal American system. Radical feminism held the assertion that all women are oppressed by men, and seeking to reform the essentially corrupt system would do nothing to eradicate the sexism. Radical feminism held the basic institutions of marriage, family, and religion as accomplices in the oppression of women.

Primary Document Excerpts

"Toward a Female Liberation Movement"

By Beverly Jones and Judith Brown, Part II by Judith Brown

*In 1968, Beverly Jones and Judith Brown of Gainesville Women's Libera-
tion published what would be known as "The Florida Paper," and be
regarded as the first theoretical framework for the women's movement.
Criticizing the foundering leadership of the New Left, "Toward a Female
Liberation Movement" seemed to provide focus and motivation for the
struggle for women's liberation.*

The SDS Experience—a Female View

For a moment it will be helpful to review the experience of a young
woman who enters a radical movement, unmarried, to appreciate her
position against the backdrop of male movement behavior. For we
should recognize clearly the conditions under which we live as oppressive in order to identify ourselves with other women in a common
struggle.

The typical "radical" woman goes to college and is well-endowed intellectually, physically, and sexually. She has most likely excelled somewhere in high school, whether as a scholar, politico, or artist. She is fully capable of competing with men in college work, and simultaneously, she has already learned that it pays to restrain those overt displays of her competency which men feel no shame in exercising. In exclusively female circles she has held leadership positions and felt bored there, and she has remarked, at least once in her life, that she "prefers the more stimulating company of men." She is not a homosexual, and she usually echos the fraternity brand of contempt for "fags" and "dikes." She thinks she is turned off to women and is secretly relieved that she passed through the "stage" of homosexuality without "becoming one." Yet, she may quietly recognize that she has loved at least one woman somewhere along the way.

At the same time, she is unusually adroit at the sophisticated forms of putting down men, and more than once she watched a movement male explaining tactics or leading a demonstration with personal knowledge that he is a bad screw or privately panders to his parents. Her nearly subliminal review of these failings would stop at mere insight were it not also true that she has, on occasions she can recall, savored her knowledge and derived malicious pleasure from it. It is this idle malicious pleasure, which in adult life finds fuller expression in a petty, indirect, consistent, and fruitless attack on men, which should be the litmus for why the woman ought to concern herself with female liberation first.

Because she knows that equality between the sexes in the movement is nonexistent. She knows, as we have said, that women are silent at meetings, or if they speak, it is slightly hysterical and of little consequence to all the others. Men formally or informally chair the meeting. Women, like all good secretaries, take notes, circulate lists, provide ashtrays, or prepare and serve refreshments. They implement plans made by men through telephoning, compiling mailing lists, painting picket signs, etc. In some quarters, now that written analysis seems to have supplanted organizing as the status movement work, women are promoted to fill that void. More often than not, however, radical women sit through meetings in a stupor, occasionally patting or plucking at "their" men and receiving, in return, a patronizing smile, or as the case may be, a glare. In demonstrations they are conspicuously protected, which does not always mean, however, they are spared the club or the jailhouse, but they are spared *responsibility* for having made the direct confrontation.

In the jailhouse, they experience perhaps the only taste of independent radical female expression given them. There, they are segregated by sex, and the someone who always assumes leadership is this time a woman. They find out about each other, probably for the first time. They learn that the others, like themselves, are generally brave, resourceful, and militant. If they stay in jail long enough, they begin to organize themselves and others in the cell-block for prison reform, etc. They get up petitions, smuggle out protest letters and leaflets, mount hunger strikes, and other forms of resistance. They manage very adequately to sustain the abuses, self-imposed disciplines, the loss of status, and the fear, which their brothers face. Outside, of course, jailhouse reminiscence is dominated by the men. And the women desegregate themselves, recalling only rarely a faint affection for their former cell-mates. It is little wonder then that for some women, jail may be the first time that they know their sisters and work with them in radical organizing *where they're at*. A very militant white woman remarked to me that after 34 years, a husband, and three children, an earlier two-month stint in jail was the first time she felt at home in organizing.

The radical woman lives off-campus, away from her parents, and often openly with one man or another. She thinks this is "freedom." But if she shares a place with a man, she "plays marriage," which means that she cooks, cleans, does the laundry, and generally serves and waits. Hassles with parents or fear of the Dean of Woman help to sustain the excitement—the romantic illusions about marriage she brought to the domicile.

If she shares an apartment with other women, it is arranged so that each may entertain men for extended visits with maximum privacy. Often, for the women, these apartments become a kind of bordello; for the men, in addition to that, a good place to meet for political discussion, to put up campus travelers, to grab a free meal, to sack out. These homes are not the centers for female political activity; and rather than being judged for their interior qualities—physical or political they are evaluated by other women in terms of the variety and status of the radical men who frequent them.

But women in general are becoming healthier, better educated, more independent, and as the years go by, more experienced movement personnel. The movement itself is growing up. The one-time single female organizer marries, and her younger sisters are beginning to see that movement participation will not save them from essentially the same sexual and marital styles they reject in their parents. The older, now married radical woman goes on trips—to visit the parents; may live in a larger, less free apartment; or may even live in a home she and her husband buy. She is "protected" by her husband, and generally she stays at home when he goes out to move the world. The marital pattern sets in, and he lapses from a sloppy courtship to ordering her to get the drinks, cut the grass, etc. The tremendous political investments made by the older radical women (now 25–30) didn't make a way for the younger; newcomer female radicals have fewer illusions these days about what is in store for them anyway, and the life-styles of their predecessors offer little inspiration. Is it surprising then that we read in radical journals that they are dropping out of the movement in droves?

Jones, Beverly, and Brown, Judith, *Toward a Female Liberation Movement*, Gainesville, FL, 1968, (full text available through http://redstockings.org/index.php ?option=com_content&view=article&id=52&Itemid=66).

The SCUM Manifesto (Society for Cutting Up Men)

By Valerie Solanas

More than any other document to come out of the radical feminist era, Valerie Solanas' The SCUM Manifesto reflected the rage which burned in so many hearts of radical feminists. From the publication of the outlandish SCUM to her attempted assassination of artist Andy Warhol, Valerie Solanas assumed the role of fringe outlaw of the movement.

Life in this society being, at best, an utter bore and no aspect of society being at all relevant to women, there remains to civic-minded, responsible females only to overthrow the government, eliminate the money system, institute complete automation and destroy the male sex.

It is now technically feasible to reproduce without the aid of males (or, for that matter, females) and to produce only females. We must begin immediately to do so. Retaining the male has not even the dubious purpose of reproduction. The male is a biological accident: the Y (male) gene is an incomplete X (female) gene, that is, it has an incomplete set of chromosomes. In other words, the male is an incomplete female, a walking abortion, aborted at the gene stage. To be male is to be deficient, emotionally limited; maleness is a deficiency disease and males are emotional cripples.

The male is completely egocentric, trapped inside himself, incapable of empathizing or identifying with others, or love, friendship, affection or tenderness. He is a completely isolated unit, incapable of rapport with anyone. His responses are entirely visceral, not cerebral; his intelligence is a mere tool in the services of his drives and needs; he is incapable of mental passion, mental interaction; he can't relate to anything other than his own physical sensations. He is a half-dead, unresponsive lump, incapable of giving or receiving pleasure or happiness; consequently, he is at best an utter bore, and inoffensive blob, since only those capable of absorption in others can be charming. He is trapped in a twilight zone halfway between humans and apes, and is far worse off than the apes because, unlike the apes, he is capable of a large array of negative feelings—hate, jealousy, contempt, disgust, guilt, shame, doubt—and moreover, he is *aware* of what he is and what he isn't.

Although completely physical, the male is unfit even for stud service. Even assuming mechanical proficiency, which few men have, he is, first of all, incapable of zestfully, lustfully, tearing off a piece, but instead is eaten up with guilt, shame, fear, and insecurity, feeling rooted in male nature, which the most enlightened training can only minimize; second, the physical feeling he attains is next to nothing; and third, he is not empathizing with his partner, but he is obsessed with how he's doing, turning in an A performance, doing a good plumbing job. To call a man an animal is to flatter him; he's a machine, a walking dildo. It's often said that men use women. Use them for what? Surely not pleasure.

Eaten up with guilt, shame, fears and insecurities and obtaining, if he's lucky, a barely perceptible physical feeling, the male is, nonetheless, obsessed with screwing...He'll screw a woman he despises, any snaggle-toothed hag, and furthermore, pay for the opportunity. Why?...

Completely egocentric, unable to relate, empathize or identify, and filled with vast, pervasive, diffuse sexuality, the male is psychically passive. He hates his passivity, so he projects it onto women, defines the male as active, then sets out to prove that he is (prove that he is a Man). His main means of attempting to prove it is screwing...Since he's attempting to prove an error, he must "prove" it again and again. Screwing, then, is a desperate compulsive, attempt to prove he's not passive, not a woman; but he *is* passive and *does* want to be a woman.

Being an incomplete female, the male spends his life attempting to complete himself, to become female. He attempts to do this by constantly seeking out, fraternizing with and trying to live through a fuse with the female, and by claiming as his own all female character- istics—emotional strength and independence, forcefulness, dynamism, decisiveness, coolness, objectivity, assertiveness, courage, integrity, vitality, intensity, depth of character, grooviness, etc.—and projecting onto women all male traits—vanity, frivolity, triviality, weakness, etc. It should be said, though, that the male has one glaring area of superi- ority over the female—public relations. (He has done a brilliant job of convincing millions of women that men and women and women are men). The male claim that females find fulfillment through mother- hood and sexuality reflects what males think they'd find fulfilling if they were female...

Solanas, Valerie, *SCUM (Society for Cutting Up Men) Manifesto*, New York, 1967, (full text available at http://www.womynkind.org/scum/htm).

"Kinder, Kuche, Kirche as Scientific Law: Psychology Constructs the Female"

By Naomi Weisstein

In her groundbreaking paper, Naomi Weisstein—jokester, musician, psychologist, and writer—challenged the assumptions held by most male psychologists in the 1960s about the nature of women, saying the psychology of women is simply not known. She asserted that these assumptions were theories based on no evidence, which ignore the role of oppressive social context which most women had to endure.

It is an implicit assumption that the area of psychology which concerns itself with personality has the onerous task of describing limits of human possibility. Thus when we are about to consider the liberation of women, we naturally look to psychology to tell us what liberation would mean: what would give women the freedom to fulfill their own intrinsic natures. Psychologists have set about describing the true natures of women with a certainty and a sense of their own infallibility rarely found in the secular world. Bruno Bettelheim, of the University of Chicago, tells us (1965) that "we must start with the realization that, as much as women want to be good scientists or engineers, they want first and foremost to be womanly companions of men and to be mothers." Erik Erikson of Harvard University (1964), upon noting that young women often ask whether they can "have an identity before they know whom they will marry, and for whom they will make a home," explains somewhat elegiacally that "much of a young woman's identity is already defined in her kind of attractiveness and in the selectivity of her search for the man (or men) by whom she wishes to be sought . . . " Mature womanly fulfillment, for Erikson, rests on the fact that a woman's "somatic design harbors an 'inner space' destined to bear the offspring of chosen men, and with it, a biological, psychological and ethical commitment to take care of human infancy." Some psychiatrists even see the acceptance of woman's role by women a solution to societal problems. "Woman is nurturance . . . ," writes Joseph Rheingold (1964), a psychiatrist at Harvard Medical School, "anatomy decrees the life of a woman . . . when woman grows up without dread of their biological functions and without subversion of female doctrine, and therefore enter upon motherhood with a sense of fulfillment and altruistic sentiment, we shall attain the goal of a good life and a secure world in which to live it."

These views from men who are assumed to be experts reflect, in a surprisingly transparent way, the cultural consensus. They not only assert that a woman is defined by her ability to attract men, they see no alternative definitions. They think that the definition of a woman in terms of a man is the way it should be; and then they back it up with psychosexual incantation and biological ritual curses. A woman has an identity if she is attractive enough to obtain a man, and thus, a home; for this will allow her to set about her life's task of "joyful altruism and nurturance" . . .

The central argument of my article, then, is this: Psychology has nothing to say about what women are really like, what they need and what they want, especially because psychology does not know. I want to stress that this failure is not limited to women; rather, the kind of psychology which has addressed itself to how people act and who they are has failed to understand, in the first place, why people act the way they do, and certainly failed to understand what might make them act differently . . .

In brief, the uselessness of present psychology (and biology) with regard to women is simply a special case of the general conclusion: one must understand the social conditions under which women live if one is going to attempt to explain the behavior of women. And to understand the social conditions under which women live, one must be cognizant of the social expectations about women.

How are women characterized in out culture, and in psychology? They are inconsistent, emotionally unstable, lacking in strong conscience or superego, weaker, "nurturant" rather than productive, "intuitive" rather than intelligent, and, if they are at all "normal", suited to the home and family. In short, the list adds up to a typical minority group stereotype of inferiority. (Hacker 1951): if they know their place, which is in the home, they are really quite loveable, childlike, loving creatures. In a review of the intellectual differences between little boys and little girls, Eleanor Maccoby (1966) has shown there are no intellectual differences until about high school, or, if there are, girls are slightly ahead of boys. At high school, girls begin to do worse on a few intellectual tasks, such as arithmetic reasoning, and beyond high school, the achievement of women now measured in terms of productivity and accomplishment drops off even more rapidly. There are a number of other, non-intellectual tests which show sex differences: I chose the intellectual differences since it is seen clearly that women start becoming inferior. It is no use to talk about women being different but equal: all of the tests I can think of have a "good" outcome and a "bad" outcome. Women usually end up at the "bad" outcome. In light of social expectations about women, what is surprising is not that women end up where society expects they will; what is surprising is that little girls don't get the message that they are supposed to be stupid until high school; and what is even more remarkable is that some women resist this message even after high school, college, and graduate school.

My article began with remarks on the task of the discovery of the limits of human potential. Psychologists must realize that it is they who are limiting discovery of human potential. They refuse to accept evidence, if they are clinical psychologists, or if they are rigorous, they assume that people move in a context-free ether, with only their innate dispositions and their individual traits determining what they will do. Until psychologists begin to respect evidence, and until they begin to look at the social contexts within which people move, psychology will have nothing of substance to offer in this task of discovery. I don't know what immutable differences exist between men and women apart from differences in their genitals; perhaps there are some other unchangeable differences; probably there are a number of irrelevant differences. But it is clear until social expectations for men and women are equal, until we provide equal respect for men and women, our answers to this question will simply reflect our prejudices.

Weisstein, Naomi: *Kinder, Kuche, Kirche as Scientific Law: Psychology Constructs the Female*, Boston: New England Free Press, 1968.

"The BITCH Manifesto"

by Joreen (Jo Freeman)

Under the pen name Joreen, writer and political analyst Jo Freeman takes perhaps the most commonly used derogatory term about women and turns it into a badge of courage for the feminist movement. The essay invites women to embrace the term as an indication that women were beginning to shatter their demure, dependent, and submissive societal role—the essential goal of the women's liberation movement. Written in the fall of 1968, this paper was first published in Notes from the Second Year, edited by Shulamith Firestone and Anne Koedt, in 1970.

BITCH is an organization which does not yet exist. The name is not an acronym. It stands for exactly what it sounds like.

BITCH is composed of Bitches. There are many definitions of a bitch. The most complimentary definition is a female dog. Those definitions of bitches who are also homo sapiens are rarely as objective. They vary from person to person and depend strongly on how much of a bitch the definer considers herself. However, everyone agrees that a bitch is always a female, dog, or otherwise.

It is also generally agreed that a BITCH is aggressive, and therefore unfeminine (ahem). She may be sexy, in which case she becomes a Bitch Goddess, a special case which will not concern us here. But she is never a "true woman."

Bitches have some or all of the following characteristics:

(1)   Personality. Bitches are aggressive, assertive, domineering, over-bearing, strong-minded, spiteful, hostile, direct, blunt, candid, obnoxious, think-skinned, hard-headed, vicious, dogmatic, competent, competitive, pushy, loud-mouthed, independent, stubborn, demanding, manipulative, egoistic, driven, achieving, overwhelming, threatening, scary, ambitious, tough, brassy, masculine, boisterous, and turbulent. Among other things. A Bitch occupies a lot of psychological space. You always know she is around . . . You may not like her, but you cannot ignore her.

(2) Physical. Bitches are big, tall, strong, large, loud, brash, harsh, awkward, clumsy, sprawling, strident, ugly. Bitches move their bodies rather than restrain, refine, and confine their motions in the proper feminine manner. They clomp up stairs, stride when they walk and don't worry about where they put their legs when they sit. They have loud voices and often use them. Bitches are not pretty.

(3) Orientation. Bitches seek their identity strictly thru themselves and what they do. They are subjects not objects. They may have a relationship with a person or organization, but they never marry anyone or anything; man, mansion, or movement. Thus Bitches prefer to plan their own lives rather than live from day to day, action to action, or person to person. They are independent cusses and believe they are capable of doing anything they damn well want to. If something gets in their way, well, that's why they become Bitches. If they are professionally inclined, they will seek careers and have no fear of competing with anyone. If not professionally inclined, they still seek self-expression and self-actualization. Whatever they do, they want an active role and are frequently perceived as domineering. Often they do dominate other people when roles are not available to them which more creatively sublimate their energies and utilize their capabilities. More often they are accused of domineering when doing what is considered natural by a man.

A true Bitch is self-determined, but the term "bitch" is usually applied with less discrimination. It is a popular derogation to put down uppity women that was created by man and adopted by women. [The term] served the social function of isolating and discrediting a class of people who do not conform to the socially accepted patterns of behavior.

BITCH does not use this word in a negative sense. A woman should be proud to declare she is a Bitch, because Bitch is Beautiful. It should be an act of affirmation by self and not negation by others. Not everyone can qualify as a Bitch. One does not have to have all of the above three qualities, but should be well possessed of at least two of them to be considered a Bitch. If a woman qualifies in all three, at least partially, she is a Bitch's Bitch. Only Superbitches qualify totally in all three categories and there are very few of those. Most don't last long in this society.

The most prominent characteristic of all Bitches is that they rudely violate conceptions of proper sex role behavior. They violate them in different ways, but they all violate them. Their attitudes towards themselves and other people, their goal orientations, their personal style, their appearance and way of handling their bodies, all jar people and make them feel uneasy. Sometimes it's conscious and sometimes it's not but people generally feel uncomfortable around Bitches. They consider them aberrations. They find their style disturbing. So they create a dumping ground for all who they deplore as bitchy and call them frustrated women. Frustrated they may be, but the cause is social not sexual.

What is disturbing about a Bitch is that she is androgynous. She incorporates within herself qualities traditionally defined as "masculine" as well as "feminine." A Bitch is blunt, direct, arrogant, at times egoistic. She has no liking for the indirect, subtle, mysterious ways of the "eternal female." She distains the vicarious life deemed natural to woman because she wants to live a life of her own.

Our society has defined humanity as male, and female as something other than male. In this way, females could be human only by living vicariously thru a male. To be able to live, a woman has to agree to serve, honor, and obey a man and what she gets in exchange is at best a shadow life. Bitches refuse to serve, honor, or obey anyone. They demand to be fully functional human beings, not just shadows. They want to be both female and human, which makes them social contradictions. The mere existence of Bitches negates the idea that a woman's reality must come through her relationship to a man and defies the belief that women are perpetual children who must always be under the guidance of another.

Freeman, Jo, "The BITCH Manifesto," *Notes from the Second Year, Shulamith Firestone* and *Anne Koedt*, eds., 1970, (full text at http://scriptorium.lib.duke.edu/wlm/bitch).

Bibliography

Articles

"A Feminist Look at Children's Books," in *Radical Feminism*, Anne Koedt, ed., New York: Quadrangle Books, 1973.

Allen, Martha Leslie, "The Development of Communication Networks among Women, 1963–1983," *History of Women's Media*, Women's Institute for Freedom of the Press, 1988.

Alpert, Jane, "Mother Right: A New Feminist Theory," *MS. Magazine*, 1974.

Asbury, Edith Evans, "Women Break up Abortion Hearing: Shouts for Repeal of Law Force Panel to Move," *New York Times*, February 14, 1969, 42.

Barrett, Brian, and Grossberger, Lewis, "Women Invade Abortion Hearing," *Newsday*, February 14, 1969.

Basile, Joe, *The David Susskind Show*, WNET.org, February 3, 2010.

Birney, Catherine H., "The Grimke Sisters: Sarah and Angelina Grimke," Westport, CT: Greenwood Press Publishers, 1969, 140.

Brown, Judith, "Origins of Consciousness-raising in the South: Gainesville or Tampa?," 1986.

Brownmiller, Susan, "Everywoman's Abortions: 'The Oppressor is Man,'" *The Village Voice*, March 27, 1969.

Brownmiller, Susan, "Speaking out on Prostitution, " *Notes from the Third Year*, 1971, 75.

Bunch, Charlotte, "Lesbians in Revolt," *The Furies Lesbian/Feminist Monthly*, vol. 1, January 1972, 8–9.

Cisler, Lucinda, "Abortion Law Repeal: (sort of) a Warning to Women"; 1969.

Clark, Alfred E., "Five Women Protest 'Slavery of Marriage,' " *New York Times*, September 24, 1969, 93.

Cohen, Abby J., "A Brief History of Federal Financing for Child Care in the United States," *The Future of Children*, 5 (2), Summer/Fall 1996.

Crary, David, "Marriage: More Men Get Financial Boost," *Associated Press*, January 19, 2010.

Davidson, Sara, "An Oppressed Majority Demands Its Rights," *Life Magazine*, 1969.

Densmore, Dana, "A Year of Living Dangerously," *Feminist Memoir Project*, Voices from Women's Liberation, New York: Three Rivers Press (Crown Publishers), 1998.

Densmore, Dana, "On Celibacy," *No More Fun & Games, A Journal of Female Liberation*, Cambridge, MA: Cell 16, 1 (1), October 1968.

Dunbar, Roxanne, e-mail message to the author, November 8, 2009.

Dunbar, Roxanne, "Outlaw Women: Chapters from a Feminist Memoir in Progress," *The Feminist Memoir Project: Voices from Women's Liberation*, New York: Three Rivers Press, 1998.

Dunbar-Ortiz, Roxanne, "Native American Tribe" (e-mail), January 10, 2010.

Fagan, Patrick, Rector, Robert E., and Noyes, Lauren R., "Why Congress Should Ignore Radical Feminist Opposition to Marriage," The Heritage Foundation, 1995–2004.

Firestone, Shulamith, "The Jeanette Rankin Brigade: Woman Power? A Summary of Our Involvement," *Notes from the First Year*, June 1968.

Firestone, Shulamith, "The Women's Rights Movement in the U.S.A.," *Notes from the First Year*, The New York Radical Women, 1968.

Flavin, Jeanne, "The Real Issue Being the Abortion Debate," Open Forum, *San Francisco Chronicle*, November 24, 2008, B5.

Fox, Margalit, "Mary Daly, a Leader in Feminist Theology, Dies at 81," *New York Times*, January 6, 2010.

Freeman, Jo, "The Building of the Gilded Cage," *Notes from the Third Year*, New York: Radical Women, 1971, 139.

Freeman, Jo aka Joreen, "The Tyranny of Structurelessness," *Berkeley Journal of Sociology*, vol. 17, 1972–1973, 151–65.

Goudreau, Jenna, "Top Paying Jobs for Women," *Forbes*, January 29, 2007.

Hanisch, Carol, "The 1968 Miss America Protest: The Origins of the 'Bra-Burning Moniker,' " *The Feminist Memoir Project: Voices from Women's Liberation*, New York: Three Rivers Press, 1998.

Hanisch, Carol, "The Personal is Political," *Notes from the Second Year*, 1970.

Hanisch, Carol, "Two Letters from the Women's Liberation Movement," *Feminist-Memoir Project: Voices from Women's Liberation*, New York: Three Rivers Press (Crown Publishers), 1998, 198.

"Jane Alpert's Bail in Bomb Plot Declared Forfeited," *New York Times*, May 15, 1970, 1.

Jones, Beverly, and Brown, Judith, *Toward a Female Liberation Movement*, 1968, Gainesville, FL.

Joreen, "The Bitch Manifesto," *Notes from the Second Year*, 1970.

Joreen, "Trashing: The Dark Side of Sisterhood," *MS.* Magazine, April 1976, 59–61, 92–98.

Kaplow, Susi, "Getting Angry," *Notes from the Third Year*, 1971.

Kesselman, Amy, "Our Gang of Four," *The Feminist Memoir Project: Voices from Women's Liberation*, New York: Three Rivers Press, 1998.

King, Mary, and Haden, Casey, "Sex and Caste: A Kind of Memo," *Liberation*, April 1966, 47.

Klemesrud, Judy, "It Was a Special Show—and the Audience Was Special Too," *New York Times*, February 17, 1969, 39.

Koedt, Anne, "The Myth of the Vaginal Orgasm," *Notes from the First Year*, 1969, 11.

Lorino, Gabi, "Radical Women: Exhibit Chronicles Ways UF Women Put Gainesville on the Liberation Map," *Florida: Magazine of the Gator Nation*, Winter 2009.

Martin, Brian, "Academic Scapegoats," *Zedek*, 7 (3), August 1987, 476–81.

Miele, Alfred, "Gals Squeal for Repeal, Abort State Hearing," *Daily News*, February 14, 1969.

Morrison, Toni, "What the Black Woman Thinks about Women's Lib," *New York Times Magazine*, August 1971, SM14.

Omolade, Barbara, "Sisterhood in Black and White," *The Feminist Memoir Project: Voices from Women's Liberation*, New York: Three Rivers Press, 1998.

Radicalesbians, *The Woman Identified Woman*, 1970.

Rothstein, Vivian, "Questions Continued" (e-mail), October 16, 2009.

Rothstein, Vivian, "The Magnolia Street Commune," *Boston Review*, 1998.

Rush, Florence, "Women in the Middle," *Notes from the Third Year*, 1971.

Sapolsky, Robert M., "Girls Are Good at Math, Too," *San Francisco Chronicle*, October 20, 2009, A11.

Sarachild, Kathie, "Consciousness-Raising: A Radical Weapon," *Feminist Revolution*, Random House, 1978, 144–50.

Schad-Somers, Susanne P., "Jane Alpert Defense," *New York Review of Books*, 29 (1), March 18, 1982.

Seghi, Laya Firestone, Shulamith Firestone (e-mail), September 7, 2009.

Shepard, Richard, "Warhol Gravely Wounded in Studio," *New York Times*, June 4, 1968, 1, 36.

Tax, Meredith, "Woman and Her Mind: The Story of Everyday Life," *Notes from the Second Year*, 1969.

United States Court of Appeals for the Fifth Circuit, March 4, 1969, 7 (408 F.2d228; U.S. App.Lexis 13419; 70 L.R.R.M. 2843; 1 Fair Empl. Prac.).

Wallace, Michele, "To Hell and Back: On the Road with Black Feminism in the 1960's and 1970's," *The Feminist Memoir Project: Voices from Women's Liberation*, 1998, New York: Three Rivers Press.

Weigand, Kate, Barbara Winslow, *Voices of Feminism Oral History Project*, Northampton, MA: Sophia Smith Collection, Smith College, 2004.

Weisstein, Naomi, "Days of Celebration and Resistance: The Chicago Women's Liberation Rock Band, 1970–1973."

Weisstein, Naomi, "Kinder, Kuche, Kirche as Scientific Law: Psychology Constructs the Female," Boston, New England Free Press, 1968.

Weisstein, Naomi, "Power, Resistance, and Science," *New Politics*, Winter 1997.

Willis, Ellen, "Forward," Echols, Alice, *Daring to Be Bad, Radical Feminism in America, 1967–1975*, Minneapolis: University of Minnesota Press, 1989.

Winslow, Barbara, "Primary and Secondary Contradictions in Seattle: 1967–1969," *The Feminist Memoir Project: Voices from Women's Liberation*, New York: Three Rivers Press, 1998.

Books

Alpert, Jane, *Growing Up Underground*, New York: Citadel Press, 1990.

Atkinson, T-Grace, *Amazon Odyssey*, New York: Link Books, 1974.

Bacciocco, Edward Jr., *The New Left in America: Reform to Revolution, 1956–1970*, Hoover Institution Press, Stanford, CA: Stanford University Press, 1974.

Bair, Deirdre, *Simone de Beauvoir: A Biography*, New York: Summit Books, 1990, 388.

Berkeley, Kathleen C., *The Women's Liberation Movement in America*, Westport, CT: Greenwood Press, 1999.

Bernard, Jessie, *The Future of Marriage*, New York: World Publishing, 1972.

Bowley, Lisa, *Listen Up*.

Brown, Rita Mae, *Rita Will: Memoir of a Literary Rabble-Rouser*, New York: Bantam Books, 1997.

Brownmiller, Susan, *Against Our Will: Men, Women, and Rape*, New York: Simon and Schuster, 1975.

Brownmiller, Susan, *In Our Time*, New York: Dial Press, 1999.

Ceballos, Jacqueline Michot, *Interview with Rosalyn Fraad Baxandall*, Cambridge: The Radcliffe Institute for Advanced Study, 1991.

Chesler, Ellen, *Margaret Sanger and the Birth Control Movement in America*, New York: Simon & Schuster, 1992.

Chessman, Caryl, *Trial by Ordeal*, Englewood Cliffs, NJ: Prentice-Hall, 1955.

Clecak, Peter, *Radical Paradoxes*, New York: Harper & Row Publishers, 1973.

Coalition Task Force on Women and Religion, *The Women's Bible*, Seattle, 1974.

Daly, Mary, *Beyond God the Father: Toward a Philosophy of Women's Liberation*, Boston, Beacon Press, 1973.

Daly, Mary, *The Church and the Second Sex*, New York: Harper & Row Publishers, 1968.

De Beauvoir, Simone, *The Second Sex*, New York: Alfred A Knopf, 1952.

Diggins, John Patrick, *The Rise and Fall of the American Left*, New York, W. W. Norton & Company, 1992.

Diner, Helen, *Mothers & Amazons*, Garden City, NY: Anchor Press, 1973.

Dunbar-Ortiz, Roxanne, *Red Dirt: Growing Up Okie*, New York: Verso, 1997.

DuPlessis, Rachel Blau, and Snitow, Ann, *The Feminist Memoir Project: Voices from Women's Liberation*, New York: Three Rivers Press, 1998.

Echols, Alice, *Daring to be Bad: Radical Feminism in America*, 1967–1975, Minneapolis: University of Minnesota Press, 1989.

Evans, Sara, *Personal Politics: The Roots of Women's Liberation in the Civil Rights Movement and the New Left*, New York: Knopf, 1979.

Firestone, Shulamith, *The Dialectic of Sex*, New York: William Morrow and Company, Inc., 1970.

Freeman, Jo, *The Politics of Women's Liberation,* New York: David McKay Company, Inc., 1975.

Friedan, Betty, *Life So Far: A Memoir*, New York: Simon & Schuster, 2000.

Friedan, Betty, *The Second Stage,* New York: Summit Books, 1981.

Friedan, Betty, *The Feminist Mystique*, New York: W. W. Norton & Company, 1963, 33.

Furchtgott-Roth, Diane, and Stolba, Christine, *The Feminist Dilemma*, LaVergne, TN: Aei Press, 2001.

Gallagher, Maggie, *The Abolition of Marriage*, Hartford, CT: Yale University Press, 1996.

Gilligan, Carol, in *a Different Voice: Psychological Theory & Women's Development,* Cambridge, MA: Harvard University Press, 1981.

Greer, Germaine, *The Female Eunuch,* New York: McGraw-Hill, 1971.

Heath, G. Louis, *Vandals in the Bomb Factory, The History and Literature of the Students for a Democratic Society,* Metuchen, NJ: The Scarecrow Press, Inc., 1976.

Hennessee, Judith, *Betty Friedan: Her Life*, New York: Random House, 1999.

Hershberger, Ruth, *Adam's Rib.*

Hull, N. E. H., and Hoffer, Peter Charles, *Roe v. Wade: The Abortion Rights Controversy in American History*, Witchita: University of Kansas Press, 2001.

Kohn, George C., *Dictionary of Historic Documents*, New York, Facts on File, 1991.

Marks, E., and Courtivon, I. de, eds., *New French Feminists: An Anthology*, Brighton: Harvester Press, 1981.

Miller, Bradford, *Returning to Seneca Falls*, Hudson, NY: Lindsfarne Press, 1995.

Millet, Kate, *Sexual Politics: A Manifesto for Revolution*, Garden City, NY: Doubleday & Company, Inc., 1970.

Mills, C. Wright, *The Power Elite*, New York: Oxford University Press, 1999.

Moi, Toril, *Simone de Beauvoir: The Making of an Intellectual Woman*, Oxford: Blackwell, 1994, 24.

Moraga, Cherrie, and Anzaulda, Gloria, *The Bridge Called My Back: Writings by Radical Women of Color,* 2001.

Morgan, Robin, *Sisterhood Is Powerful: An Anthology of Writings for the Women's Lib Movement,* New York: Random House, 1970.

O'Beirne, Kate, *Women Who Make the World Worse and How Their Radical Feminist Assault Is Ruining our Families, Military, School, and Sports*, New York: Sentinel, 2006.

Orenstein, Peggy, *School Girls: Young Women, Self-Esteem, and the Confidence Gap*, New York: Anchor Books, 1995.

Pipher, Mary, *Reviving Ophelia: Saving the Selves of Adolescent Girls,* New York: Putnam, 1994.

Priesand, Rabbi Sally, *Judaism and the New Woman*, New York: W. W. Norton & Company, 1996.

Richards, Ann, *Manifesta: Young Women, Feminism, and the Future*, New York: Farrar, Straus, and Giroux, 2000.

Roiphe, Katie, *The Morning after: Sex, Fear, and Feminism on Campus*, Boston: Little, Brown and Company, 1993.

Rubin, Eva R, *The Abortion Controversy: a Documentary History*, Westport, CT: Greenwood Press, 1994.

Scanlon, Jennifer, *Jo Freeman (1945–), Significant Contemporary American Feminists: A Biographical Sourcebook*, Westport, CT: Greenwood Press, 1999, 104–10.

Shulman, Alix Kates, ed., *Red Emma Speaks: Selected Writings and Speeches*, New York: Vintage, 1972.

Siegel, Deborah, *Sisterhood Interrupted*, New York: Palgrave McMillan, 2007.

Solanas, Valerie, *SCUM Manifesto*, New York, 1967.

Stetson, Dorothy McBride, *Women's Rights in the USA, Policy Debates and Gender-Roles*, New York: Garland Publishing, Inc., 1997, 34.

Summers, Christina Hoff, *The War Against Boys*, New York: Simon & Schuster, 2007.

Thoreau, Henry David, *Walden and Civil Disobedience*, New York: Penguin Books, 1849.

Tooley, James, *The Miseducation of Women*, Chicago: Ivan R. Dee, Publisher, 2003.

Ulrich, Laurel Thatcher, *Well Behaved Women Seldom Make History*, New York: Alfred A. Knoff, 1990.

Walker, Lenore, *The Battered Woman*, New York: Harper & Row, 1980.

Weigand, Kate, *Barbara Winslow, Voices of Feminism Oral History Project*, Northampton, MA: Sophia Smith Collection, Smith College, 2004.

Websites

American Experience, People & Events: The 1968 Protest, 1999–2001, www.pbs.org/wgbh.amex/missamerica/peopleevents/e_feminists.html.

Baer, Freddie, About Valerie Solanas, www.womynkind.org/valbio/htm.

Barbara Winslow, PhD, associate professor, Adolescence Social Studies and BC Women's Studies Program, March 2009, www.depthome.brooklyn.cuny.edu.

Bridle, Susan, No Man's Land, *EnlightenNext Magazine*, 1998, www.enlighten next.org.

Bromberg, Sarah, *Feminist Issues in Prostitution*, (presentation), International Conference on Prostitution, 1997, www.feministissues.com.

Brown, Jenny, Gainesville-area Women's Liberation Movement pioneers honored in NYC, Febraury 1998, www.afn.org

Brownmiller, Susan, An Informal Bio, 2009, www.susanbrownmiller.com.

Brownmiller, Susan, Papers, 1935–2000: A Finding Aid, www.oasis.lib.harvard.edu.

Celebrate Equality Day, August 26, www.nwhm.org/home/equalityday.html.

Center for Women's Global Leadership, 2009, www.cwglrutgers.edu.

Consciousness-Raising: A Radical Weapon, Feminist Revolution, New York: Random House, 1978, 144–150, www.scriptorium.lib.duke.edu.

Dixon, Marlene, The Rise and Demise of Women's Liberation: A Class Analysis, 1977, www.marxist.org.

Fifteenth Anniversary of the Violence Against Women Act, by the President of the United States, A Proclamation, Barack Obama, September 15, 2009, www.whitehouse.com.

Guttmacher Institute, Alan F. Guttmacher, 1898–1974, 2008, www.guttmacher
    .org/about/alan-bio.html.

Hanisch, Carol, Introduction, *The Personal Is Political*, January 2006,
    www.scholar.alexanderstreet.com.

Henwood, Doug, Two Redstockings Interviewed, January 24, 2002,
    www.leftbuisnessobserver.com.

Highlights from NOW's Forty Fearless Years, 2006, www.now.org/history/
    timeline.html.

Holland, Alison T., *Simone de Beauvoir and the Women's Movement*, University of
    Northumbria, February 28, 2002, www.well.ac.uk/cfol/simone.asp.

Interview with Casey Hayden, Washington University Digital Gateway Texts,
    May 15, 1986, www.digital.wustl.edu.

Interview with Vivian Rothstein, student activist, United States, Young Blood,
    1950–1975 www.pbs.org, wgbh/peoplescentury/episodes/youngblood/
    rothsteintranscript.html.

Linder, Douglas O., The Chicago Seven Conspiracy Trial, www.law.umkc.edu.

Linder, Douglas O., "Susan B Anthony: A Biography," http://www.law.umkc.edu/
    faculty/projects/ftrials/anthony/defargument.html.

McEldowney, Carol, and Poole, Rosemary, "A Working Paper on the Media," *Women:
    A Journal of Liberation*, Spring, 1970, 40, www.wifp.org/womensmediach3
    .html.

Millet Farm, www.katemillett.com.

Millett, Kate, *An Encyclopedia of Gay, Lesbian, Bisexual, Transgender, and Queer Cul-
    ture*, 2002, www.glbtg.com/literature.

Morgan, Robin, The Demon Lover: On the Sexuality of Terrorism, 1989, http://
    en.wikipedia.org/wiki/Robin_Morgan.

Population Distribution by Age, Race, Nativity, and Sex Ratio, 1860–2005, www
    .infoplease.

Population of the United States (1860), www.civilwarhome.com.

Radical Element Feminist, 2009, www.marydaly.com.

Rhoades, Brandi, The Story of Mary King and Casey Hayden, October 2, 2008,
    www.famous-activists.suite101.org.

Robin Morgan, 2006, www.robinmorgan.us.

Roxanne Dunbar-Ortiz, feminist, revolutionary, historian, www.reddirtsite.com.

Sachs, Andrea, "Rita Mae Brown: Loves Cats, Hates Marriage," *Time* Magazine,
    March 18, 2008, www.time.com/time/arts/0,8599,1723482,00.html.

Scanlon, Jennifer, Jo Freeman (1945–), 1999, www.jofreeman.com.

Shulamith Firestone, March 4, 2009, www.perry.mindsay.com, shulamith
    _firestone.mws.

Ter, Cheryl, "Jane: Abortion and the Underground," Women News Section, *Chicago
    Tribune* Online, September 1999, www.cwluherstory.com/CWLUFeature/
    TribTheater.html.

The CWLU Herstory Website, www.cwluherstory.org.

The Furies, The Rainbow History Project, www.rainbowhistory.org.

Ti-Grace Atkinson, Tufts University, People, Faculty, www.ase.tufts.edu.

Warren, Larkin, Q & A with Kathie Sarachild, "1968: The Year That Rocked Our
    World," May 2008, www.aarpmagazine.org.

Index

("f" indicates a figure)

Abortion, 64–68
Abortion Law Repeal: (sort of) a
    Warning to Women (Cisler),
    55, 66
Abortion panel picketing,
    Redstockings, 54
"Action" efforts, 34
Adams, Abigail, xxi
African Americas: racial vs. gender
    discrimination, 30–31; and
    women, xix–xx
Against Our Will (Brownmiller), xii,
    64, 68, 109, 110
Allen, Martha, 15
Allen, Pam, 25, 34
Alpert, Jane, xi, xxvii, 26, 33, 42,
    97–101
American Women's Suffrage
    Association (AWSA), xxii–xxiii

Anarchists, xxviii
Anthony, Susan B., x, xxiii,
    xxivf, 10
Antiaborption forces, 67, 68
Atkinson, T-Grace, 15, 22,
    24, 26, 27, 35–36, 41, 101–2;
    NYC Marriage License Board
    demonstration, 57
Autonomous women's
    movement, 25

"Back-alley" abortions, 66, 86
Backlash, conservative, 87–89
Baxandall, Rosalyn, 3, 10, 37, 50, 52,
    53, 54, 96, 102–3
Berkeley, Kathleen, 30
Beyond God the Father (Daly), 19,
    112, 113–14
Biren, Joan E., 38, 40

Bitch Manifesto, The (Freeman), 12–13, 17, 122, 152–54
Black women/white women, conflict, 30–32
Blackwell, Elizabeth, xxv
Bloomer, Amelia, xxv
Blue Stockings, 35
Booth, Heather Tobias, 24, 104–7, 129
Boston's Women's Health Collective, 72
Bra burning myth, 51
Bromberg, Sarah, 75
Brown, Judith, 8, 9, 30, 33
Brown, Rita Mae, 22, 38, 39, 62, 107–9
Brownmiller, Susan, 36, 60, 64, 68–69, 73, 74, 109–10
"Building of the Gilded Cage" (Freeman), 17, 80
Bunch, Charlotte, 38, 40–41, 110–12

Camp Hastings conference, workshops, 32–35
Carmichael, Stokely, 5
Ceballos, Jacqui, 52
Celibacy, 70–71; as alternative, 8; Cell 16, 28, 35
Cell 16, Boston, 28–29, 35, 58
"Chicago Eight" trial, 56
Chicago Women's Liberation Rock Band, 58–59, 136
Chicago Women's Liberation Union (CWLU), 8, 23–24, 24f, 128, 129
Child care: campaigns, 77; government-sponsored, 11
Children's books, sexism in, 16
Choice, and feminism, 95–96
Chronology, xv–xvii
Church and the Second Sex, The (Daly), 19, 112, 113

Cisler, Lucinda "Cindy," 55, 66
Civil Rights Law (1964), xxxii
Clarenbach, Kay, 21
Clecak, Peter, 90
Clinton, Hillary, 89
Coleman, Corinne, 25, 35
Congress of Racial Equality (CORE), xxxiv
Consciousness-raising, xi, 25, 26, 33; African American response, 31; approaches, 34
Conservative backlash, 87–89
Consumer materialism, xxxi, xxxii
Contraception, 11, 71–72
Cronan, Sheila, 25, 26, 28, 35, 53
Cultural feminism, xii, 27, 28, 39, 41–42, 77–78
Czolgosz, Leon, xxix

Daly, Mary, 3, 19, 42, 75, 79, 112–14
Daring to Be Bad (Echols), 93
Das Kapital (Marx), xxvii
David Susskind Show, 52
Davidson, Sara, 95
DC Women's Liberation, 53
de Beauvoir, Simone, x, 1–4, 2f
Debs, Eugene, xxviii
Declarations of Rights and Sentiments (Stanton), xxii
Deevey, Sharon, 38, 40
Democratic 1968 Chicago Convention, 56
Democratic capitalism, xxvii
Densmore, Dana, xxvii, 3, 28, 29, 35, 58, 73, 114–16
Dialectic of Sex, The (Firestone), xii, 11–12, 118, 119
Diana Press, 78
Dixon, Marlene, 30, 31, 34, 54
Dobbins, Peggy, 25
Douglass, Frederick, xxi

Duffett, Judith, 47
Dunbar, Roxanne, xxvii, 28, 49,
    53–54, 116–18
Dworkin, Andrea, 73, 120
Dylan, Bob, xxxiv

Echols, Alice, 76–77, 78, 93
Economic dependency, de Beauvoir
    on, 3–4
Economic oppression, Firestone
    on, 11–12
Education, feminist impact on,
    92–93
Emancipation Proclamation, xxi
Engels, Frederich, xxvii
Ephron, Nora, 60
Equal Employment Opportunity
    Commission (EEOC), 21,
    22, 81, 82
Equal opportunity, 75–77
Equal Rights Amendment (ERA),
    xii, xxvi, 85–86
Equality feminists, 41
Erikson, Erik, 5

Family equals social patriarchy,
    Millett, 13
Far Left, xxvii
Feminine Mystique, The (Friedan),
    4–5
Feminist Issues in Prostitution
    (Bromberg), 75
"Feminist Look at Children's Books,
    A," 16–17
Feminist Memoir Project, 106,
    116, 124
Feminist press, 15
Feminists, The, 26, 27
Firestone, Laya, 33
Firestone, Shulamith, xxvi, 10,
    11–12, 23, 25, 35, 53, 61, 118–20;

on Jeannette Rankin Brigade, 46;
    on nuclear family, 77
First Congress to Unite Women, 58
First Wave Feminism, x, xxvi
Flagg, Fannie, 109
Fox-Genoee, Elizabeth, 94
Free Space (Allen), 34
Free Speech Movement, Berkeley,
    xxxiii
Freedom Trash Crash, 50, 51
Freeman, Jo, 12, 13, 17, 23,
    80, 120–23
Freud, Sigmund, 10
Friedan, Betty, x, 4–5, 18, 21, 22, 26;
    Dunbar debate, 52–53; "lavender
    herring," 36
Fuller, Margaret, xxi
Furies Collective, 38–39

Gainesville Women's Liberation,
    8, 30, 33
Gang of Four, Chicago, 106, 128, 129
Gardner, Jennifer, 25
Garrison, William Lloyd, xx
"Getting Angry" (Kaplow), 16
Giardina, Carol, 8, 30
Gilman, Charlotte Perkins, xxxi
Ginsburg, Ruth Bader, 83
Goldman, Emma, x, xxviii–xxx
"Goodbye to All That" (Morgan),
    14, 126
Gould, Lois, 73
Griffiths, Martha, 81
Grimke, Angelina, xx
Grimke, Sarah, xx
Griswold vs. Connecticut, 71, 87
Griswold, Estelle T., 71
Guerilla street theater, 29

Hanisch, Carol, 10, 30, 42, 50, 90,
    123–25

Hart, Lois, 62
Hayden, Casey, 6, 7
History of Women's Media
    (Allen), 15
House Un-American Activities
    Committee (HUAC), xxxiii
Hyde Amendment, 67–68

Illegal abortion, 67
Industrial/International Workers of
    the World (Wobblies), xxviii, xxxi

JANE, abortion referral network,
    25–26, 66, 104, 105–6
Jeannette Rankin Brigade,
    45–46, 46f
Jimenez, Rose, 67
Jones, Beverly, 8, 9

Kaminsky, Barbara, 35
Kaplow, Susi, 16
Kearon, Pam, 12, 26, 35
Keefe, Terry, 3
Kesselman, Amy, 106, 129
"Kinder, Kuche, Kirche as Scientific
    Law: Psychology Constructs the
    Female (or the Fantasy Life of the
    Male Psychologist)," 10, 149–51
King, Martin Luther, Jr., xxii
King, Mary, 6, 7
Knights of Labor, xxviii
Koedt, Anne, 10, 16, 25, 26,
    35–36, 70
Komisar, Lucy, 60
Kritzler, Helen, 33

Labor movement, xxvii
Labor protection laws, 17
Ladies' Home Journal sit-in,
    59–60, 60f
"Lavender Menace," xi, 36, 61–62

Lesbian-feminist communes, 40–41
Lesbianism, as alternative, 8; de
    Beauvoir on, 3; as divisive issue,
    14, 36–38; NOW's stand, 22, 36;
    as political choice, 38, 40
"Lesbians in Revolt" (Bunch), 38–39,
    110–11
Liberal feminism, xii, 18, 41,
    42, 77, 91
Liberator, The (1831), xx
Lilith, Seattle, 15
"Loving Another Woman"
    (Koedt), 16
"Lyrical Left," xxviii, xxxii

Madison Square Bridal Fair protest,
    WITCH, 47
Mainardi, Patricia, 25–26
Making of an Intellectual Woman, The
    (Moi), 3
Malcolm X, xxxiii
"Man-Hating" (Keamon), 12
March, Artemis, 37, 62
Marriage, Brownmiller on, 69
Marriage, de Beauvoir on, 3
Masses, The, journal, xxxi
Maternalism, 42
Maternity, de Beauvoir on, 3;
    Firestone on, 11
McCall's 19, 20
Media Women, 59–60
Mehroff, Barbara, 26, 35
Millett, Kate, xi, 13, 37, 39,
    52, 125–26
Miss America 1968 protest, NYRW,
    49–52, 51f
Mobilization Committee to End the
    War in Vietnam (MOBE), Nixon
    counter-inauguration
    demonstration, 53
Moi, Toril, 3

Morgan, Robin, 14, 18, 29, 50, 72, 126–28
Morning After, The: Sex, Fear and Feminism on Campus (Roiphe), 70
Morrison, Toni, 31
Mother Earth, radical feminist journal, xxx
Mother Right (Alpert), 42, 98–99, 100–101
Mott, Lucretia, xxi
Ms., pronoun use, 94
MS. magazine, 17–19, 91, 92
Muller v. Oregon, 80
Murray, Pauli, 21, 22
"Myth of Vaginal Orgasm, The" (Atkinson and Koedt), 35–36, 70

National Conference on New Politics, 23
National Organization for Women (NOW), xi, 5, 21–23, 91; image concerns, 26–27; lesbian support, 39–40; New York chapter, 22, 26
National Woman Suffrage Association (NWSA), xxiii
National Women's Liberation Conference: 1st, 30; Camp Hastings, 32–35
National Women's Party, xxvi, 86
National Women's Rights Convention, Seneca Falls, xxi–xxii
New Left, xxxi–xxxv; and autonomous women's movement, 25; feminist criticism, 6–7, 8; women's movement separation, 56–58
New York City Marriage License Board demonstration, 57, 69
New York Radical Feminists (NYRF), 25, 26, 33; Speak Out on Rape, 63–64

New York Radical Women (NYRW), 10, 12, 15, 25, 118, 124, 126, 129; Miss America 1968 protest, 49–52, 51f; "Traditional Womanhood" demonstration, 46
Newsweek, sex discrimination charges, 61
19th Amendment (Susan B., Anthony Amendment), xxv–xxvi
Nixon, Richard, inauguration demonstration, 53
No More Fun and Games, Cell 16 journal, 19
North Star, abolitionist newspaper, xxi
Notes from the First Year, 10, 46, 118
Notes from the Second Year, 12, 15, 66
Notes from the Third Year, 15, 74, 80, 109, 122, 123

Off Our Backs, Washington, D.C., 15
Olivia Records, 78
Omolade, Barbara, 32
On Women's Right to Vote (Anthony), xxiii
"Oppressed Majority Demands Its Rights, An" (Davidson), 96
Our Bodies, Ourselves, 72

Palin, Sarah, 89
Paul, Alice, xxvi, 86
Pegrebin, LettyCottin, 17
"Penis envy," de Beauvoir on, 4
"Personal is political," 42, 90
Peslikis, Irene, 25, 35
Playboy Bunny demonstration, Seattle Radical Women, 47
"Politicos," New Left feminists, xi, 4, 26, 33–34
Politics of Housework, The (Mainardi), 26

Pornography, 72–74

"Post-Christian Radical Feminism," Mary Daly, 19

Priesand, Sally, 78, 79

Private property, and patriarchy, 4

Prostitution, 74–75

Prostitution Papers, The (Millett), 126

Protection laws, 80

Psychology, Weisstein on, 10, 11

Quest, The: A Female Journal, 78, 111

Radical feminism, ix–x, 77; decline, 42, 90–91, and lesbian-feminist alliance, 39; impact of, 92–96

Radical People's Constitutional Convention, 2nd, 38

Radicalesbians, 37, 111

Rape Crisis and Domestic Violence Centers, 69

Rape, 68–70; Millett on, 14, 18, 68

RAT Subterranean News, 14

Red Scare, xxx

Redstockings, xi, 18, 35–36, 118, 125, 129; "Speak-out on Abortion," 54–55, 65

Reed v. Reed, 83

Reed, Sally, 83

Religion, Daly on, 19, 42, 79

"Resistances to Consciousness-raising" (Peslikis), 25

Roberts, Sylvia, 82

Rockefeller, Abby, 28

Roe v. Wade, xii, 25, 67, 86–87

Roiphe, Katie, 70, 94

Rothstein, Vivian, 24, 128–29

Rubyfruit Jungle (Brown), 109

Sanger, Margaret, x, xxv, 72

Sarachild (Amatniek), Katie, 10, 18, 30, 33, 34, 42, 62, 129–30

Schafly, Phyllis, 87–88

SCUM Manifesto, The (Solanas), xii, 48, 70, 131, 146–48

Seattle Radical Women (SRW), Playboy Bunny demonstration, 47

Second Congress to Unite Women, 36, 37, 61–62

Second Sex, The (de Beauvoir), x, 1–4

Second Wave Feminism, x, xxvi

Separatism, 27

"Sex and Caste: A Kind of Memo" (King and Hayden), xi, 6–7, 30, 106

Sex discrimination: in law, 83; organized religion, 78–79; pay, 80, 81; workplace, 80, 81–83

Sexual Politics (Millett), xii ,13–14, 39, 125

Sexuality, Firestone on, 11, 12

Shelley, Martha, 62

Sisterhood is Powerful (Morgan), 126

Slave revolts, xx

Snow, Lucy, xxiii

Social constructionism, 11

Socialism, xxvii, xxviii, xxx

Solanas, Valerie, xi, 48, 49f, 70, 131–33

Speak Out on Abortion, Redstockings, 55

Speak Out on Rape, NYRF, 63–64

"Speaking Out on Prostitution" (Brownmiller), 74

St. George, Katherine, 81

Stanton, Elizabeth Cady, x, xxi, xxii, xxiii, xxivf, xxv, 10

Steinham, Gloria, 18, 91

Stowe, Harriet Beecher, xxi

Student Nonviolent Coordinating Committee (SNCC), xxxii, xxxiii–xxxiv, 5–6

Students for a Democratic Society
    (SDS), xxxii–xxxiii, xxxiv, 6
Sudsofloppen, San Francisco, 34
Suffrage movement, x, xxi–xxiii

"Take Back the Night," 70
Tax, Meredith, 75–76
"Therapeutic abortion," 66
Things Which Are Done in Secret
    (Dixon), 54
Third Wave Feminism, xiii
Time Magazine, sex discrimination
    charges, 61
Title VII, Civil Rights Act of 1964,
    81, 82
"Toward a Female Liberation
    Movement," 8–9, 143–46
"Traditional Womanhood"
    demonstration, NYRW, 46
Truth, Sojourner, xxi
Tubman, Harriet, xxi

Uncle Tom's Cabin (Stowe), xxi
Universal suffrage, xxiii, xxv

Vietnam War opposition, 45
Violence Against Women Act, 70
Voice for Women's Liberation,
    The, CWLU newsletter, 24,
    120, 121
Voting Rights Law (1965), xxxii

Wage gap, 80
Walker, Mary, xxv
War, and patriarchy, 4

War on Poverty, Lyndon B. Johnson,
    xxxii
Weathermen, xxxiv, 56–57
Webb, Marilyn, 33, 53
Weeks v. Southern Bell, 82
Weeks, Lorena, 82
Weisstein, Naomi, 8, 10, 58, 106,
    129, 135–37
White women/black women,
    conflict, 30–32
Willis, Ellen, 18, 35, 41, 92,
    94–95, 118
Winslow, Barbara, xxvii, 47–48,
    133–35
WITCH (Women's International
    Terrorist Conspiracy from Hell),
    xi, 25, 29–30, 126, 127; Madison
    Square Bridal Fair protest, 47
Woman Against Pornography
    (WAP), pornography conference,
    73f, 73–74
"Woman-Identified Woman, The"
    (Radicalesbians), 37–38, 111
Woman's Bible, The (Stanton), xxv
Women & Art, 25
"Women in the Middle," Florence
    Rush, 16
Women rabbis, 79
Women's businesses, 77, 78
Women's Page, The, 25
Women's Strike Coalition, 37
Women's Strike for Equality, NY
    NOW, 62, 63f
Woodhull, Victoria, xxvii
Workers unions, xxvii

About the Author

PAUL D. BUCHANAN is a professional social worker and licensed counselor, with an MA degree in counseling, and an MFT license, living in San Mateo, California. Mr. Buchanan has written "Famous Animals of the States," "Historic Places of Worship," "Race Relations in the United States: A Chronology, 1896–2005," and "The American Women's Rights Movement: A Chronology of Events and Opportunities from 1600–2008."